CrowHeart

becoming unwounded

a memoir of transformation

Keelin Anderson

For an unwounded hand may handle poison.

-The *Dhammapada* of The Buddha

Why a memoir?

I dream I am in the bedroom of a teenager. *It is not a bedroom I recognize but it is mine. I feel an insect land on my arm. In reflex, I brush it off into the bedclothes. I do this a few times before I realize there is a butterfly landing on my forearm. I see I am being given a gift. A grasshopper lands alongside the butterfly. I feel love and gratitude. I go into the living room. I tell all my family members present that they must be careful not to kill the grasshopper and butterfly. I love these creatures so much. I explain I understand insects are small and humans large, that they might be killed accidently and I accept this. I move into the kitchen. My grandmother and mother are doing the dishes. I call for their attention. I cannot get their attention. The butterfly lands on my mother's back. I am sure my mother will swat at the butterfly and kill her. I rescue the butterfly in time, back onto my forearm. My mother turns around, surprised. She says she usually doesn't like insects landing on her but this was okay. I go back into my bedroom. Anna, in this dream my sister, lies on my bed reading my diary. I feel threatened, exposed. I think to tell her to stop reading, that it is private. Then I realize if Anna needs to read my diary, my most private experience, in order to evolve, I accept this. My willingness to say in public, "This is true," is part of my job.*

Claiming Lost Children

I journey in meditation. *I find her in one of those airport chairs attached to all the other chairs in a row, her feet dangling over the edge of the 1970s orange plastic. I sit beside her, and before us a large gray window looks out over the tarmac. We can see the baggage cars parked ziggedy-zagged like a child's train, the jet way's cave door gaping into space. She wears a flowered full-length cotton dress her paternal grandmother made her for Christmas, an envelope safety-pinned to her shoulder. She sits quietly, still, watching the uniformed woman at the counter, the planes going by out the window. She is six years old.*

Her mother told her not to talk to strangers, to be careful not to let them take her away. She is to sit where the flight attendant in the blue uniform told her to until someone else comes to get her. Her mother and her mother's boyfriend, Mr. Dean (she is supposed to call him Mr. Dean even though he lives with them), put her on the airplane alone in Peoria. Now she waits alone in Chicago for the airplane to Los Angeles.

Her parents divorced when she was two years old. Her father lives in Los Angeles. Her mother did not ask her if she wanted to fly by herself to California to see her father for the summer. This is the way it is. She is not afraid because being afraid when there is no one to help you is intolerable. She has taught herself to be quiet, to listen

2

carefully to instructions by adults, to know which adults are safe to ask for help, and to hide where she is told to wait. She hides well. She is good at not drawing attention to herself.

I sit down next to her. I tell her she doesn't have to do this anymore. She never has to do this again. She never has to be alone again; she has me. She can stay with me as long as she wants. I ask her if she needs anything. She asks to be held. I pick her up and hold her. In my body, reclining in a chair at the therapist's office, I sob uncontrollably. It seems I cannot stop, my diaphragm in spasm making it hard to breathe. I shake all over. *My six-year-old self loves me. I feel how much she loves me and I love her so much. She is perfect, beautiful, brave, smart. She says she wants to leave the airport. I ask where she wants to go. She wants to go with me. She wants a puppy or a pony. I take her to a field where she can have a pony. She hugs the pony's thick, shaggy neck. She joyfully brushes his long bushy mane.*

I have done similar meditations many times. I have an emotion in the present: anxiety, fear, anger, grief. I feel a tightness in the belly, a blank spot in the chest. I go to that place and see what is there, first with the guidance of an NLP (neurolinguistic programming) hypnotherapist, then a craniosacral therapist, an acupuncturist, and later, on my own. For the first few years, such meditation work brings up intense feelings of grief and strange body sensations. I sob uncontrollably, cannot breathe, cannot lie still, shake all over, cough deeply, feel tingling and numbness in different parts of my body, my pelvis, my nose, my chest.

I journey in meditation. *I find my fetus self in the womb. It is a lonely place; no one is here with me. I feel abandoned here and angry about being sent yet again into a life. I already dread this childhood. My mother feels absent to me. How will I survive? I must grow my first tender cells in the womb alone, the base nutrients my cells need to reproduce the only nourishment. I remember love. I enter this life knowing how to love. Already I recognize its absence. This woman does not know how to love. How could that be? To love is as easy and natural to me as moving my fingers and toes, kicking my tiny feet. I am confused, bewildered. I remember the path of life here on the Earth. I have to get through all my basic, vulnerable growth without love. How will I do that? It is too much. I want to go back to God. I am fiercely angry with God for this. A part of me decides not to play along. I will endure, but I won't participate. This part isolates itself, resentful and closed up, like a seed with a protective shell and a bitter taste.*

My adult self, sitting in the therapist's office, recognizes this dissociated part. I see this leaving of my body became a habit, and the resulting despair and depression a familiar companion. *I catch my newborn self from the womb and hold her as she takes her first breaths. I put her to my breast and feed her, nourish her, love her. I thank her for her courage, her wisdom, her fierce protection of what she knows about love.*

With practice, over time, the impulse to go to the child and care for her becomes more immediate. I can respond by myself, wherever I am, to her emotions coming through my adult life. When she is triggered, I immediately ask what she needs. I am driving to the beach by myself. I feel anxious. My sternum tightens up. I think something bad will happen. I imagine I will have an accident, be attacked, raped, if I dare leave home. I interrupt the self-scare thoughts and find my little girl, whichever age is present. While I drive I invite her onto my lap and hold her. I say I love her. I tell her we are safe. She is safe. She doesn't have to do anything she doesn't want to. I ask her if she is afraid to go on this trip today. I tell her she doesn't have to go. I ask what she wants to do. She says she doesn't want to go but after a moment she changes her mind. She wants to go because she wants to be with me, to play with me, and we are going to the beach to play, to have a day for us. A few miles down the road she is no longer present. I forget my anxiety; the tight feeling around my heart lessens. I relax into the seat. Driving along, I look forward with joyful anticipation to the sand and the ocean. I notice the autumn light on the wheat fields, the angled shadows across the wooded hills, a red-tailed hawk on a fence post.

I Do Not Have To Be Good

I think this will be easy. I am not afraid of heights and I have a harness on. I can fall into the harness anytime, just like rock climbing, and I love climbing to high places. The pole, a log like a telephone pole, has steps, metal rungs to climb. I quickly scamper up. I am supposed to stand on the top, thirty feet in the air, and jump off, caught by the harness. I find the trick at the top: a metal disc that rocks in place. I pull myself up to standing and find I cannot steady myself – the disc keeps tilting under my feet. My legs are shaking. I am confused. I am not scared, but my legs are shaking. I cannot control them. I start to panic. The leader of the challenge calls out, "Keelin, don't be so hard on yourself!" and I laugh. I realize I feel embarrassed that my legs are shaking and afraid when I cannot control them. I decide to wait, take a few deep breaths, slow down. A few moments later my legs stop, I am okay. I can stand on the tilting disc on the pole with ease. I jump off into the air.

On the ground, elated, I see how my body responds to a little patience. I don't need to control what I cannot control in my body. I need to make some space and time for my body to adjust herself and adapt. She may need to move to adjust, shake a little to express the fear I have hidden so well I do not even realize I have it. I glimpse an intelligence to my body I had not noticed before. She knows what she is doing. For the first time I feel a spark of kinship with my body. We can help each other.

It is December 2006; I am at a spa resort in Tucson, a ten-day gift with and from my mother. I am thirty-six years old. I do all the challenge course exercises and yoga classes. I learn Mindful Eating, Mindful Decision Making. I spend a lot of time in the hot tub. At the spa I try Reiki, Craniosacral Therapy, Trager, and Chi Nei Tsang. I have had Swedish massage before but never other types of bodywork. Right from the first session of Reiki, I start to lose it. Each time I am on the bodywork table, no matter the therapy, I sob and cry. I'm horrified, anxious, and relieved at the same time. When someone touches me with love and gentleness, male or female, I cry like an infant left alone on a rain-drenched doorstep. The power of the feelings terrifies me. It feels like it will never stop; and simultaneously, the relief of being myself, of being witnessed as myself, of letting out feelings I have not been able to express, no matter how inappropriate, inexplicable, or crazy, is immense.

I dream the women I work with are drunk, at a party. *I don't want to party. I leave. A woman is in my truck, in the driver's seat. We start to drive down the road and I see she is drunk. I'm furious. I wrestle her away from the driver's seat into the back seat. I take over driving my truck. The steering is hard to control. The brakes barely work. I am able to slow the truck but we careen down the road like a bobsled, barely missing the cars coming toward us in the other lane. On a curve of the highway, I carefully stop for a child sitting in the gravely dirt on the side of the road. She has black skin. She is beautiful. I go to pick her up, to rescue her from the side of the highway and she stops me. She reaches back down to pick a flower. I start to say, "No! Dirty!" but she lifts the flower to show me how beautiful it is. She smells it, her face joyful and unafraid.*

A wire is strung between two telephone poles. Tied to a rope hitched to the center of the wire, I am hoisted up to the top of the first pole. I hold tight to a rope that keeps me in place. When I let go I will swing down toward the ground thirty feet below me. I can stay here where I know I am safe but cannot move, or I can let go and see what happens. I let go and scream all the way down. I see how my old habits, old ways of keeping safe and in control, obscure my ability to see my life and myself as it is and to move forward. I always have to guess what I want because I am not in my body to feel what I want. This dissociative habit keeps me out of my body like the drunk woman in my dream. Even though I don't know how else to live, I don't want her running my life anymore. Even though it seems I cannot steer or brake, I need to drive my own truck. I need to let go of what I know by habit and try something new.

Again, I think this will be easy. I climb up the rungs on a telephone pole to stand on a log thirty feet in the air. Safely harnessed in case I fall, I am to walk across the log to the other side. I find I cannot take the first step. I am afraid to let go of the pole. I wait, take a few deep breaths, and am still afraid. Prompted by the cheering of my fellow participants below me, I simply start walking. I am scared all the way across and yet I walk across. On the ground once again I am full of joy. I feel lighter, freer. It is okay to be afraid. I can be afraid and still move forward. I realize I have been more afraid of having fear than anything in the world I might actually fear. I hate being afraid, hate myself for feeling constant anxiety. I feel intense shame when I cannot control my body or my emotions. I never learned how to have fear, how to cope with it. I am learning now. Perhaps I could make room for fear, make friends with it, carry it with me.

Home from Tucson, I consciously practice being kind to my body. In meditation, I feel my feet. *I say, "Thank you feet for taking such good care of me, for supporting me, for connecting me to the Earth." I work my way up. "Thank you uterus, you work so beautifully, preparing my body for creation again and again, so I will be ready to grow life, you clean yourself and build a nest anew. Thank you heart for remembering who I am through everything. We are safe now and you can open. Thank you lungs. You remember freedom and possibility. You never forget how to relax. Teach me now. We are safe. We can relax." Each organ seems like a miracle. They work so hard for me and I sense they are innocent, diligent, loyal. I feel this up-welling of love for each part of my body. I speak to my anxiety, my constant companion stuck in my chest. "Thank you fear for keeping me safe for so long. We survived. We are safe now. You have done a brilliant job and you can rest now. We can all rest now...."*

Two weeks later, my mother has surgery. She asks me to stay the first few days with her in the hospital. Unexpectedly, the hospital does not have cots for visitors to spend the night. I try to sleep in a chair and then on the arctic floor. I find not being able to sleep to be nearly unbearable as my anxiety is at its worst in the middle of the night. Still awake at four am, I am furious at myself for getting into this situation. I find I cannot take care of my mother.

In the pain, fear, and stress of being in the hospital, she seems to me like a child. She wants me present to comfort her and keep her safe. I can't do it. She is an adult. She has been an adult since I came into the world. She was not present to comfort my fears or keep me safe when I was a child and I resent it. I realize in agreeing to help her through this situation I have agreed to put her needs above my own. This is a trend in our relationship and I cannot do it any longer. It means I silence myself, and my mother need not face her own fears and the consequences of her decisions. I apologize to her for changing my mind, but I cannot stay with her. I go home to get some sleep and take care of myself. I visit her in the hospital a few times during the week until she can go home.

At the Buddhist meditation hall in my neighborhood I listen to a talk about compassion. The speaker makes a plea for all of us to think of others more than ourselves. I feel intense stabs of hurt and shame for leaving my mother in the hospital. I have to speak up. During the Q&A, I say, "I think sometimes the most compassionate act I can do for another person is to say no. If their need requires me, at the cost of my own integrity, to protect them from facing the consequences of their decisions and actions, it may be better to refuse."

The conversation continues to a discussion of emptiness. The consensus seems to be that it means a negation of self such that you go around doing whatever anyone asks of you. This sounds like dissociation and I think they have it all wrong. My inklings of emptiness come from going further into myself, not away. I'm beginning to realize compassion comes from being fully home and present in my body as an ordinary human being. I have more empathy and love for others the more empathy and love I feel for myself. And this means I speak up for myself more than I used to, not less. Like the Mary Oliver poem about the wild geese where she says all I have to do is to allow my body to love whatever it loves, I think compassion for others flows naturally from compassion for myself.

It All Makes Sense

Lying on the table, I am tense and shaking. The craniosacral therapist has one hand above and one hand below my left hip. Her hands are mostly still, occasionally shifting position, pressing in, or moving my body. I am crying. *I see myself as an infant, pressed down on my left side, a hand holding down the right side of my head. A man, my father, is having sex with my baby body. The hand on my head feels comforting, loving. In my adult body on the table I feel aroused and freaked out. I need to get out of here, be alone, away from other people.*

I find a local craniosacral therapist, Rita, on the web. My second appointment falls during the week my mother recovers in the hospital. In the session I realize for the first time that I was sexually abused as an infant. After the initial fear, I mainly feel relief. All of the sudden so much about my life makes sense. My need to sob like a baby makes sense. I was hurt as a baby. I have extreme anxiety when I cannot sleep at night, and intense irritation when woken from sleep. My father woke me at night for the abuse. Memories start falling into place: my deep mistrust of my father; my predisposition for being sexually abused as an older child, my constant anxiety, wariness, and vigilance into adulthood; my need to fill my mouth with sweets and food; my fantasies about being hurt or raped and then finding safety in a male protector, the father I wish I'd had; my tendency to dissociate from my body during sex or stressful events; my need for absolute control of my body, my emotions, and my life, to feel safe.

I have many habits from post-traumatic stress. I begin to consciously work to let these go. When I get caught up in controlling my life, I work with my mind, telling myself, *"Thank you Scheduler for taking care of me. We don't need to plan everything anymore. We are safe. You can rest now. Thank you Vigilance for taking such good care of me. I love you. We don't need to prepare for the worst anymore. We are safe. You can rest now. Thank you Irritation for taking such good care of me. We are no longer in danger. You have worked diligently to warn me of trouble. We are safe now. You can rest."*

I work with my body in meditation to relax overworked protection mechanisms: *"Thank you adrenals for taking such good care of me. You have worked tirelessly for my survival through the worst, preparing for possible danger again and again. We are safe. You can rest now. Thank you pericardium. I love you. You have been a shield of iron to protect my heart. We are safe now. You can loosen, relax, unwind, learn to move, expand. My heart needs room to grow now. We are safe. You can rest."*

I begin a conscious process of validating my own experience and knowledge. Incest taught me not to trust myself. My father said he would not hurt me while he hurt me, so I learned to doubt my own experience of pain. This fundamental insecurity, learned before I could talk, has hampered my ability to trust my own feelings and experiences my whole life. Others' opinions, my mother's, my husband's, my therapist's, have often been louder in my head than my own. Not only have I not been able to say no to sex, I have stifled my voice in other areas of my life out of fear and insecurity.

Staci Haines explains, in *The Survivor's Guide to Sex*, that healing from sexual abuse requires a woman to become her own point of reference for the truth. She must trust her own perceptions and truths over messages from the outside. I am the only person who can measure the impact incest has had on my life. I need to own what I know and take responsibility for what I need. Spiritual growth, an internal process, requires me to validate my own experience. No one else lives in this body with me. I feel called to grow in this way, so I must learn to trust myself. I tape a Zen Card to the front of my journal as a reminder.

The card is about loyalty, about staying true to your course even if you are the only one on the path.

I dream my mother wants to walk on the beach. *She asks where I want to go. I tell her but she doesn't want to go that way. We walk the beach her way. The waves are too big, dangerous, crashing over the rocks at us. We have to run. She looks back and yells, "My boot! My boot!" Her sandal is in the water. I go into the dangerous surf, get her sandal and hand it to her.*

I dream I am going to sleep. *Something blows out the candles. There is a dog in the room. It is pitch black. I try to yell to tell the dog that I am there but I can't yell. I need to yell something, say* something, *before the dog bites my face but I am choking. I can't use my throat. I'm terrified. The dog jumps on the bed, growling.* I call out in my sleep, waking my husband. He wakes me up. He says, "You're safe."

I dream I am at Disneyland. *I agree to carry a small disabled young man named Roger on my shoulders while I roller skate around the park. He seems to trust me not to fall but he is also jaded, cynical about our chances. The Disney employees treat him like a special guest, like he is the son of the owner of the park. I tell him how I remember some of the things I did here as a child. He says they weren't that much fun. They were kind of stupid.*

Through January, my mother and I exchange emails. It is as if we are both talking to a wall. My wall is consciously made, a boundary to protect the small space I have carved out for my perspective that differs from hers. Her wall is unconscious, what I believe to be a narcissistic blindness that ignores anything that does not get her what she needs. She cannot hear me. We are both angry and hurt and the emails just make it worse. I ask her to switch to snail mail, hoping that without the cyberspeed our communications will be more cautious and considered, less knee-jerky.

In *Anatomy of the Spirit*, Caroline Myss points out that a parent can rape a child's energy field such that the child is unable to live and grow separate from the control of that parent. My mother needs me to need her. She does not wish me to be an independently powerful individual. I forgive her in that I am not interested in hurting her further or hashing out the litany of complaints about my childhood with her. I can deal with those feelings on my own and I do. But forgiving her does not mean I will allow her to hurt me further by silencing my current experiences or feelings. I will not do what she wants if there are negative consequences for my life, my health, and my own spiritual and emotional well-being.

I speak to a condescending woman at the Buddhist center. She says I will understand things someday like she does, when I have meditated and studied for years. I am irritated. She doesn't recognize me as brilliant and spiritually aware so I don't like her. Myss explains that our judgments of other people are attempts to take power from them. Later, upon reflection, I imagine someday, when I inhabit myself more fully, I may be able to listen to this woman with neutrality, to listen without needing anything from her. I imagine hearing what she has to say so deeply that I see why she says it, understanding in the moment the truth behind her words. This woman needs to think herself more enlightened than me. This attitude is about external power. She needs to feel superior and I don't want to feel inferior. We are struggling for power between us. I am trying to get power my parents stole from me by stealing from others. This is an endless cycle. I need to find my own power, internal power, to realize the power I have always been since before I came into the world.

In meditation I say, *"Critic, I love you. You have kept me safe for a long time, trying to regain power I have lost and given away. We are safe now. We have our own power. We do not need to steal from others. Rest and relax. Be at peace now. Thank you Guilt. You want to care for our mother. You want to respond to her suffering. It is an honor to feel love and empathy for her."*

My father is dead. He died of lymphoma a few years before the time of this memoir. When I was twelve years old, living in Ohio with my mother, my father sold all of his possessions in Los Angeles and moved to Rajneeshpuram, in central Oregon, to live with other followers of the Bhagwan Shree Rajneesh (now known as Osho). This move marked the end of my solitary summer visits with my father. From then on, I talked to him on the phone perhaps once a year and saw him every three or four years. He died in New Mexico, where he moved to live with a patient/girlfriend from his psychiatric practice after losing his medical license in Washington. They were trying to open a Reiki healing center. By the time he died, my father had told me on three separate occasions that he had finally reached enlightenment.

I have a set of Rajneesh Neo-Tarot Cards [Osho Cards] that my father sent me from "The Ranch". A reading consists of pulling five cards, one each for: the problem, what to let in, what to let go of, the solution, and one for "Bhagwan's Insight". While I have a healthy suspicion of gurus and cults from watching my father navigate the New Age, I have learned more from these cards than from any other source of spiritual wisdom.

Mid-January, on a lovely surprise day of snow, I do a reading:

Problem: **Becoming Centered** – A courtesan fails to sway a follower of Buddha. She tries to seduce him but he remains centered and unchanged. She is so impressed she decides to become a follower as well.

Let in: **Sex** – Orgasm is a release of self into energy so sex mirrors the way to God. In orgasm, as you release separateness by love and surrender, you become One.

Let go of: **Acceptance** – A Zen Master is accused of fathering a child. He cares for the infant, saying nothing to defend his honor. When the true father is found, he gives the infant back, again without resistance.

Solution: **Disciplehood** – An old Master, asked about his greatest teacher, names three ordinary things he encountered in his travels, a dog, a thief, and a little boy, each with its own lesson. He explains his greatest teacher has been all of existence.

Insight: **Anger** – A Zen disciple, worried about his fits of anger, goes to his Master for advice. The Master asks to see the anger but the student cannot show it, he does not have it right now. The master explains that the anger, if not there all the time, cannot be a part of his core nature, so it must have come from the outside.

From the cards I understand that all of existence is pulled to God as to a magnet. Therefore the path, my path, is already going there. My hunger for God, though normal and human, is not needed to find God. The more I can **center** in and live from my heart and body, the more clearly I will know my path and **accept** what life brings. **Sex** has been my teacher, incest my teacher, suffering my teacher. I have been a **disciple** of all this experience. My father, who seems the villain in my story, will perhaps be my most effective teacher. My **anger** at him is temporary, an emotion to be expressed and allowed to pass through. I am not my emotions. This is how I forgive him. I love him for how he has served my path to consciousness. In our contract for this lifetime his role was the more difficult – to be the person who could do what he did is more painful than my path. I am able to heal within this lifetime. That is my task. My father, wherever he is, remains unhealed. Coming into this life, I never forgot how to love. Leaving this life, my father never remembered.

Abandoned in the Lovely Night

Joseph Campbell, in his interviews with Bill Moyers, said that people are not searching for meaning in life but for the *feeling* of being alive, and experience of rapture. I want to feel the rapture of being alive, but to feel, I must be present in my body. There are parts of my body I do not live in, parts I have not felt for a long time. I associate these parts with pain or vulnerability and I have closed them off to survive. I heal by moving into my body and being present in my being as a whole. As I more fully inhabit my body, I make it possible to *experience* being alive.

My sacrum rests in Rita's lower hand. Her upper hand lies over my uterus. She asks what my uterus looks like. I look: *She is a dried-up hard walnut. I see a hole in my right ovary. I think of the abortion I had when I was nineteen. At Rita's suggestion we decide to allow that pregnancy to come to term in meditative journey. I watch my uterus grow larger. She is amazingly capable. She knows exactly how to do this. She is full of red muscle, blood, warmth. The fetus has a dent in his head. His name is Brian. He grows larger, nestled safely. My belly protrudes, my breasts fill. Then he leaves, bleeds out my cervix. My uterus cleanses herself out to start again, steady in her work. I tell Brian good-bye. I feel grateful. I thought this would be sad. I thought I would feel guilty, but there is a sense of rightness. He would not have been born, whether through abortion or miscarriage. Doubt in my mind says I made this up. It may be a convenient comfort, but there is another truth present that I feel in my heart. I feel whole. I feel at home in my pelvis, present in a new way, alive there. I have new sensation there. My uterus appears healthy, full, strong, capable, creative.*

At home, I meditate, but my anxiety cannot rest. I feel new twinges around my uterus, my right ovary, little cramps and pains I have never felt before. I worry I have ovarian cancer. I tell several friends about the incest. I worry I should not have. I feel vulnerable, exposed. I regret telling them. Messages of fear buzz loudly around my head like a frantic bee. It makes me angry. I cannot control it. I hate it. Rather than feeling calm and relaxed from sitting in meditation, my tension ratchets up.

Myss suggests that becoming conscious means we shift the locus of our perceptions from the mind into the body such that we begin to live and feel what we know to be true rather than to just think it. To practice the move from my mind into my body, I try to love the anxious bee. I meet him with my heart rather than my head. He is a part of me. He wants to protect me with his ceaseless vigilance and buzzing, planning for the worst. I cannot feel love for him at this moment, but I can practice talking to him as if I loved him. Fake it till I make it. Rather than frightening myself with the bee, as I do by default, telling myself that I am in danger, that I will lose something if I don't watch myself, I change the tape. I say to the bee, *"I love you, bee. Thank you for your fierce protection. In this moment we are safe. We can cope. Let us rest now. Find a honeycomb nearby and take a seat with me. Rest your tired wings. Breathe with me. Become my friend."*

At the Buddhist center I meditate with others in silence in the sanctuary. *I breathe in pain and fear – a child punished, put in the closet in the dark, sitting on the shoes next to the vacuum, coattails brushing her head, she watches the light seeping under the bottom of the door, waiting to get out. I breathe out freedom and love – the beach in Maui, safety, the abundant warm sun on my head, turquoise water washing ankles, bare feet sinking into the sand. I see God as a light filling my body. I spread the light down through my head, through my organs one by one, out my arms and legs. The light spreads to all the others in the room till we are all connected, all glowing. The light expands, fills the in-between spaces. The light becomes a glowing sphere, expanding through the corners of the room, up over the roof, down into the soil.*

Rita asks me to pay attention to the area she is working on. I go there in my body. I ask why I should pay attention. She explains that consciousness does the work; presence does the work. When I add my attention to hers, there is more presence available. *Rita holds my head in her relaxed hands. My spinal cord is a big, healthy earthworm. I move through rich, warm dirt, cradled on all sides by all I need to live and grow, by more food than I could ever eat, by layers of earth providing absolute safety. I eat and poop freely as I tunnel along. I fall asleep on the table.*

My mother and I remain at an angry impasse in our letters. We argue in circles about each of our perceptions of my childhood. I have to stop arguing, just put the conversation down. I stop writing back with my side of the argument. I don't need to change her point of view. I want an acknowledgment that my experience may have been different from hers. She has her own version of events. She wants me to accept her version as the only version. I cannot be the daughter she wants without negating parts of myself. I cannot move into my whole being while silencing parts of who I am for my mother. I am changing, growing up. I have new boundaries.

My husband and I try to have sex. We haven't tried since I remembered being abused. I don't feel aroused. I am tense. I can't relax. I tell him I feel too tense to do this. We stop. He doesn't pressure me. He understands. I can't stop crying. I panic. I fear he will leave me because I said no to him. I feel like a child – a scared child in an adult woman's body naked in bed with her adult husband. I feel intense shame. He will fall out of love with me because my secret's out – I am just a scared little girl. I don't believe he loves me. I don't feel lovable. I upset myself into a migraine.

My feelings often seem too big, out of control, hard to hide, and irrationally unconnected to real events in my life. At times I am convinced that my feelings and needs make me unworthy of love. My inability to speak up for myself, to state my feelings and needs, to say no, stems not only from experiencing incest, but also from the effects of parental conditional love.

Elan Golomb explains, in *Trapped in the Mirror*, that a child raised by narcissistic parents is valued and loved for what she can reflect back to the parent. The child's feelings and needs are ignored so that she develops the belief that her only value comes from being what other people want her to be. The child becomes an adult with little sense of internal and intrinsic self-worth.

Since I left home, I have worked hard to create self-esteem, but this confidence vanishes when I need to contradict or deny the requests of my mother or my husband. The cause is simple. My mother could not handle when I cried. It told her she was a bad mother. So she ignored me when I cried, or told me there was no reason to cry and to stop. I learned when I cry that no one will love me. I learned to hide my feelings and needs, to behave in a certain way in order to be loved. I have known this for years – psychotherapy 101. But how do I change the belief? On a deep level, when deeply upset, I always return to it, like a broken record, convinced I am an unlovable, broken person.

Rita's fingertips rest lightly on my temples. I sob strongly for several minutes. *I see the anatomy she concentrates on, my sphenoid bone, the sella turcica, or Turkish saddle, where my pituitary gland rests above the back of my throat. The corners of the saddle are sharp, pointed, poised to stab into my brain. My soft palate, the back of my throat, feels pushed up, too high, leaving a big gaping space. I know I have been hurt here, through my throat. I feel an erotic choking. I want oblivion. I want to die like this, with my throat full.*

I tell my NLP hypnotherapist, Diane, about the sharp spikes around my pituitary, the feeling of rape in my throat. I think my migraines are related to repressed emotions and, because they are often hormonal, a conflicted relationship with my female body. During the session, with tones alternating in my ears, she tells me to ask my unconscious if I am ready to heal this. The experience is so astounding, I write her a letter:

2/11/07

I had to write to tell you that what you led me through in our last session was amazing. I feel my own unconscious moved the bones and tissues in my head to heal. Weird, amazing! How is this possible? Since the incest images came to me last month, I have had this recurrent image of the back of my throat like this open hole that would be violently stabbed until I died. And the bone under my pituitary appeared sharp and spiky.

When you had my unconscious work on it, I expected to see images or something, but I just felt like that area was sore, moving a little, like it was being scanned back and forth. I didn't see anything consciously.

Now the open vulnerable image is completely gone. When I think of that area, it seems to me that the entire back of my upper mouth has lowered into place. There is no hole there anymore. My throat feels closer in, tighter. And the area around my pituitary gland is smooth and cradling rather than sharp or threatening.... Thinking of choking on a penis, or dying from choking on it, has no emotional charge. It is not arousing or painful. It's just a thought like any other.

Anymore it seems to me that we heal ourselves. We are trained to think that we have to rely on others to heal us, but you simply suggested to my unconscious (albeit in a safe environment, with a person I trusted completely, and reinforced with bilateral stimulation) that it heal this area if it was ready to, and it did so. I find this astonishing! You didn't even touch me, you were sitting across the room. "Thank you" doesn't really do the experience justice. Wouldn't it be an amazing world if people helped each other to heal themselves routinely. Like it was readily available and happened everyday – it was just another loving thing among a billion loving things that we all experienced all the time.

In much gratitude, Keelin

During this time, my sadness feels overwhelming. I have days I cannot stop crying and I don't know why. Myss encourages her readers to look at changes in their lives, including changes in the body, as messages. So how do I respond to my changing emotions not with fear, but with curiosity? What is the message contained in my grief? I struggle for patience with these feelings. I choose an Osho card:

> **Gratitude** – A woman comes into a village at dusk looking for lodging. She is turned away. She has to sleep out in the cold, in a field, under a cherry tree. She feels sorry for herself, rejected unfairly by the villagers. She wakes in the night to the incredible beauty of the cherry blossoms under a full moon. She finds she feels intense gratitude to the villagers for refusing her lodging. If they had given her shelter, she would have missed this gift.

From the card I understand that it is my *fear* of grief that makes me want to know why I have it. I want to decide the meaning of events before they come to fruition. I don't know how to heal what I need to heal. I don't know what it will take, what I will experience. I have not walked this road before. The grief seems like being left out in the cold, alone, to fend for myself without reason or explanation. I feel sorry for myself. I take my suffering personally. I need to wait for the why. I don't know if there is a cherry tree in full bloom out here yet or not.

Going Crazy

I want to study craniosacral therapy and so enroll in massage school. Before classes begin in April, I try a weekend workshop on Reiki. Friday evening, during the introduction, the male teacher explains we will undergo three initiations to attune us to Reiki energy, the first one that evening. This man wears loose lavender pants. He reminds me of my father. He has a European sense of personal space. When I ask him a question, he gets up close to me with his body for the conversation. I feel uncomfortable.

For the first attunement, I sit in a chair in a circle with three other students, facing in. We have to close our eyes. The teacher does something over us, like hand motions, and then blows air. I don't like this at all. I make myself do it by freezing like a rabbit until I can run away. At home after class I don't want to go back. I am confused. I do not trust the teacher or understand what he is doing. I don't want to sit with my eyes closed while he does something mysterious to my body. But I have paid over three hundred dollars for the class which I forfeit if I drop out; and, I am used to making myself do things that feel wrong because I think have to or I should. I don't want to be seen as a quitter, or afraid, so in spite of my gut feeling not to go back, I think I should just go and get it over with.

I do an Osho reading to help with my confusion:

> Problem: **Self-Acceptance** – A tree wants to be beautiful like the flower. A bush wants to be tall like the tree. The tree and bush start to die. The flower, hearts-ease, is healthy and vibrant. The gardener asks why and the flower replies that she figured when the gardener planted her, he wanted hearts-ease.
>
> Let in: **Transformation** – Breathe in pain, breathe out peace. This is the tonglen meditation I learned at the Buddhist center.
>
> Let go of: **Innocence** – St. Francis of Assisi loved so completely that he could communicate with plants and animals with his heart. People thought he was crazy.
>
> Solution: **Understanding** – Two monks are crossing a river. A woman needs help getting to the other side so one monk carries her. The other monk is furious as they are forbidden to touch women. He silently fumes all the way back to the monastery. He speaks up at the door, threatening to report this incident to the Master. His companion explains that he left the woman at the river, but wonders if the other monk still carries her.
>
> Insight: **The Gates of Hell** – A samurai warrior goes to a Zen Master and asks how to get to heaven. The Master's answer is to insult the warrior's honor. Affronted, the warrior lifts his sword to kill the Master. The Master explains, looking at the sword over his head, here is the gate.

The reading tells me God wants me the way I am. Keelin is the seed God planted, so Keelin is exactly what is needed. I myself can **transform** pain into peace, right now, with **self-acceptance** and by **understanding** what my heart needs in this situation, not what my ego needs. My resistance to allowing myself to drop the class points to the burden I need to put down. Don't make this decision from ego, from the voice that is worried about wasting money or being seen as a quitter. Make this decision with self-acceptance and awareness. I am where I am in my healing. I have parts of myself like my father that I am afraid of, so I fear this teacher. The lesson here is self-compassion. Accept where you are and do what you need to do to feel safe and loved.

I realize I don't need this class. I don't want to partake of any healing rituals that are secret, that involve the specially trained having power over the uninitiated. I need to say no. The next day I go early to ask the teacher if I can have my eyes open during the Reiki initiation. I explain that it bothers me to have my eyes closed while someone does something mysterious to me. He says no. I realize he has no insight into why this might bother me. I am disappointed. He inadvertently makes the situation worse by offering for me to be initiated alone, away from the group. He says I just need to trust him. This so closely mimics an abuse scenario that I feel angry a male teacher at a massage school would not have more awareness around his female students. I decide not to finish the class.

At a busy intersection one day, a woman almost runs me over in the crosswalk. She glares at me in irritation, as if I am inconveniencing *her* and it was my fault she almost killed me. I feel angry. It occurs to me to practice tonglen meditation right here, right now with these feelings. I breathe in my anger, her irritation, and I breathe out okay, acceptance. I do this several times. By the end of the next block I have forgotten the incident. My mind has moved on to other things. I find this amazing. Usually I would stew about this for the rest of the day, my anger and sense of injustice increasing in strength and impotence. With a few moments of meditation, I have left the incident behind. I feel liberated, happy, strong, and light.

I dream: *I go to the opera by myself. The guy sitting next to me puts his shoe in my lap. Then he touches me between my legs. I tell him not to do that again. During the show my wallet is taken from my purse and returned with no credit cards or ID. There is a man and a girl waiting to drive home with me in my rental car.*

During this time I have frightening moments when I feel I don't know who I am. When I speak up for myself, after the adrenaline abates, I feel disoriented and dissociated, lost and sad. It is just like in my dream when I say no to being touched inappropriately and then I have no ID, no identity. I have these extra people riding around with me in the car, and it is not even my car but a rental car, just like the drunk woman in the back seat of my truck. I wonder when it will just be me in the truck.

The first week of March, on my thirty-seventh birthday, I have a panic attack. I fear I am going crazy. It seems everything is changing, that I have nothing to stand on, hold on to, but my external world is the same. I am panicking but don't know what I am panicking about. Rita somehow makes it make sense. She explains that as long as you can tell what day it is, who the president is, and name the town where you live, you are welcome to be as crazy as you want in other areas. Change is frightening. I no longer wish to continue as I am, stuck in patterns of self-defense and fear, but I don't yet know whom else I could be. Between the old self and the new there is a transition zone, a loss of identity, that feels horribly insecure and wrong. And I am hesitantly trying out new ideas that my old belief system categorizes as delusional.

Rita talks to animals and trees. I ask her how she does it. How do you know the language? She explains that the language, be it color or sound or image, can only be interpreted in your own personal context. You cannot ask another person how to do this. She says that all that exists is energy. How energy shows meaning to you is an internal language you have to figure out on your own. I want to believe in the possibility that I could talk to animals and trees and stones. I am also afraid of that possibility. I have to change my entire world-view, the way I define myself in relation to everything else. This is terrifying. I want to hope and fear being hopeful, fear being wrong and fooled, embarrassed and disappointed.

I share a little about my recent experiences with my husband. He seems threatened by my internal changes. He thinks people who believe in God are a little delusional, not to mention people who talk to stones and trees. We knew we had different beliefs when we married. When I met him in college at eighteen, we were both atheists at a generally atheist school. By the time we circuitously got around to getting married at thirty-two, I had found I believed in God. Until recently, we didn't talk about it much, but now God seems to be moving front and center for me. I fear at times that I will have to choose between my spiritual growth and my husband. Sometimes I think he is limited in his world-view and growth, and that I see more, know more, than he does. Other times, usually when I feel more secure, I see he is not limited. He is different. I don't know the full picture of what we are doing here but there is a reason we are together.

I seek out an experience with another craniosacral therapist to learn more about the work. I find a male therapist, Sam. The first session, he moves his hands over my heart, carefully and respectfully around my left breast. *I feel numbness and tingling in my pelvis, uterus, and ovaries. The feeling moves to my sternum and down my arms to my hands. The bridge of my nose is numb and tingly. I see a blood stain in my head in the place where I get migraine pain – a stain like my period on my underwear. I cough repeatedly. I cannot breathe. I cough deeply, contracting my ribs. After a while of feeling short of breath, I notice my need to breathe lessening. A huge relaxed space opens between my out breath and my in breath. Sam tells me to stay with what I am feeling as much as I can. I see this cone-shaped light emanating from a point behind my back out through my heart and into the world.*

Sam asks me to think about the question, "Why am I here?" I hear, "To bring God more strongly into this world." I realize I had to experience being closed up tightly to learn how to open. If I wish to help others to heal, I need to know every step of the way of opening my heart by heart. After the session I notice my sternum feels different. Grateful and amazed, I write Sam a thank you:

3/12/07

I feel like a different person. My sternum has moved, it's more rounded out now, and there is space around my heart. I feel larger there, and calmer, more open in general in my attitude and outlook. What you did with me feels like such an amazing gift... I've never had anyone touch my heart, not metaphorically, but physically touch it before. Maybe you do this every day in your practice, but I had never experienced it before, so it was profound for me, beyond me. It was like we spent time together in love but it was God love, not sex or bounded human love, and that was something I have never been aware of doing with someone else before. And because it was God love, it was abundant and given freely, that is the most amazing thing about it. That you can touch souls with someone, something I have always been desperate to do, and it can be the most normal, quotidian thing to do. Nothing desperate about it, just serene and joyful.

I learned so much in that hour of time. I can feel things in my body and live through it. I can share the most intimate thing with another human being and it can be given freely, unconditionally. That I can be open, so I feel energy, God, whatever, moving through me, and it feels right and natural, it makes so much sense, and though it frightens me – I want to spend a short time there and then run back to existence as I know it – you gave me the opportunity to spend some time there, like you were physically teaching me to meditate, to go back again to that space when my brain says no way, I will die if I stay here any longer, and I saw that I could hang with God a little longer, that my tissues, my being, could move with God and nothing cataclysmic would happen, except that I would change and grow.

Thank you so much,
Keelin

Learning to be Ordinary

During this time, I own a retired horse. Ross is injured enough to be unrideable but not so much that he cannot live out his life comfortably in a field. I endeavored to heal the injury and ride him for about two years before I said enough and turned him out to pasture (a few months before I went to the spa in Tucson). It was an agonizing decision and the loss remains painful.

I have lunch with an acquaintance from the Buddhist center. We talk about horses and Dressage. This is a type of riding where in harmony with the rider, one works for relaxation, obedience, and free movement of the horse. She tells me Dressage is a meditation practice for the Shambhala lineage. I tell her about Ross. She says she wishes she could have a horse. She says I should keep riding, that it would be a mistake to stop. Hearing this feels like a wound being pulled open and poked with a stick.

I often struggle with other people's opinions. I feel too receptive to other's judgments about my life, and I allow what they think to hurt my feelings and threaten my self-confidence on a regular basis. Golomb explains this lack of boundaries as typical for the narcissist's child forced to take in and accept the parents' opinions and worldview. Through to adulthood, thus trained, the person will digest whatever is said about them from the outside, praising or poisonous, even if it negates her own sense of self.

I find people tend to romanticize horse ownership and women dream of having a horse like they wanted to as little girls. They often have no idea what modern horse ownership and horse sports actually entail, no inking of the time investment, injury risk to rider and horse, and amount of money spent with small guarantee of return. I need to remember this: I am the only one who has lived the past five years of my life with my horses. I am the only one who can judge the joys and difficulties I have experienced.

I dream I am camping in the woods with two men. *The older one, like my father but not him, comes over to my sleeping bag as I get ready for bed. We are going to have sex but when he sees my body he mentions a book he read that I know. The book states that all fat is pathological – that if all people were mentally healthy, they'd be skinny.*

He believes this and decides not to have sex with me. This does not bother me at all. I see it as his opinion and not mine. I feel neutral about this, as if he likes the color red while I like blue. I lie on my sleeping bag with my chest revealed. I feel beautiful and confident.

He sees the glowing eyes of a large predatory cat coming in the dark toward us. He tells us we have to walk away from the camp into the woods and get up on couches and picnic tables to keep from being attacked. A large, beautiful black panther emerges from the woods and tries to bite me as I move from couch to picnic table and back. Getting up on the furniture is not keeping me safe. The father-man doesn't really know what he is doing. I end up kicking the cat in the face with my boot repeatedly as she tries to bite me. I see that I am hurting the cat, making her jaw bleed and stunning her. I ask God while I kick the cat, "Why? Why do I have to kill this beautiful animal?" Hurting animals is wrong. This is very painful for me to do. The cat is only doing what comes by instinct for her. She is innocent. The cat collapses to the ground, bleeding from the head. I feel pain for the cat, for having to kill her to live myself. She runs off but is bleeding; I know the other animals will kill her.

As I wake, a meaning comes to me. I think the panther is the part of my mind that tries to protect me by constantly coming up with improvements to the way I am (everything would be great if I just lost weight, etc.). She is my neurosis. She is innocent in that I needed her as a child to survive and she developed to help me. I was not accepted for my being and loved as I was as a child. I had to believe I could be different, be the child my mother wanted, so I could believe I was worthy of love. My father would normally trigger these neurotic thoughts, but in the dream, he does not. I am healed, whole, and feel neutral in my response to him not finding what he wants in me. In fact, I feel beautiful just lying there, regardless of his looking at me or being there.

When the cat comes to bite me, to shame me into improvement so I can be what my dad wants to love, I fight back. I don't need to be ashamed anymore. But it is painful to fight back. I am killing, rejecting, making bleed a part of myself I have needed and cherished for a long time. This is the problem with trying to eliminate neurotic thinking. I believe the thoughts are my natural, animal self, the beautiful, cleaner part of me; and rightly so because they have been my companion and savior through difficult and painful times. But these thoughts are not me. The panther is no longer needed. I am lovable as I am in this moment, no improvement needed. It hurts to heal, to reintegrate my being, to coax the panther back into her den to rest and lick her wounds. To heal takes tremendous will and courage and strength to change my beliefs about myself. What feels natural for me may not be my natural self. It may just be habit, survival habit, a comfortable and familiar self-hatred.

I am changing. I haven't cried for a few weeks now. My mood has been steadier, my negative emotional states shorter in duration. I find myself more flexible and accepting, less anxious than I can recall from memory. I have fewer panic attacks; feel able to cope more often. I have eight weeks off between ending my job at the horse equipment store and starting massage school. I fear free time and in the past often got depressed with nothing to do. This time I actively let go of the rules. I don't make myself do anything. I don't keep a schedule. I don't make myself eat a certain way or exercise on a plan.

I fear "letting myself go" and this fear keeps me locked in neurotic habit. These habits have never made my life better. I am done with them. To change my behavior, now I consciously accept the consequences of whatever I fear. I tell myself if I end up an obese, heart-diseased television addict, so be it. If that is what God wants, I will learn to be that. I start feeling out what I want to do. Rather than deciding my actions based on a set of arbitrary life rules I have made for myself, I surrender to what feels right, to the sense of being guided.

The morning of my first craniosacral workshop, I pull an Osho card: **Ordinariness**. The story is a Zen Master, asked what miracles he can perform, replies that when he is hungry, he eats, and when he is thirsty, he drinks. Osho says that the real challenge to spiritual growth is to be ordinary. The ego wants miracles, and with it, power. The true path is to follow nature without the mind interfering.

In the workshop, I learn that to do craniosacral therapy I must flow with nature. I tell my left-brain, the critical, questioning know-it-all, to take a rest for a while. I explore what happens if I don't know what I am doing ahead of time. If I sense my hands should press in to the body, I press in, if I sense they should move out, I pull them away. I practice listening to the body without deciding what I will hear. In the workshop I have permission to just go with it and see what I find. I learn craniosacral work does not happen through my special talents or magical gifts. It is tapping into, though practice, the ordinary but generally hidden inherent movement in all of our body tissues.

Learning to Grieve

I dream I work in a 1950s drug store. *I step out onto the sidewalk into a 1950s parade scene. Black and white, full-fendered cop cars follow in the parade. My grandfather walks with me. I confront him, accusing him of sexually abusing me as a child. He becomes furious and aggressive. He takes out a pocketknife to kill me. I am angry. I struggle to stop him from folding out the knife. We enter the house fighting. There are other, teen-age 1950s-*

dressed girls in the house. They are hurt in the fight. Finally I get my hands on the pocketknife. I open it and the knife locks in place. Grandfather has a big sword. It is floppy. He swings it at me but chops off the head of one of the other young women. I grab the sword and bend it away from me. I stab him in his fleshy belly with the pocketknife. I twist the knife to get him to bleed and die. He dies. The young woman picks up her head and puts it on her neck. She instantly heals.

I wake, freaked out by the violence in the dream. The break I make with my family by healing is extreme, violent. I am messing with the family code, the way it has always been. My grandfather represents a family legacy of control, abuse, and silence. In my family you don't talk back. In my family when you are abused, perhaps not physically but emotionally, mentally, the abuse is experienced as love. You take it because it may be the only love you get and it is good for you. The parents are trying to shape you into their idea of a lovable person and they don't know any better. They learned this from their parents and so on. And it is normal, perversely comfortable. It's who we are and as adults we internalize the parent and continue to struggle to make our unlovable selves better. I have always been bemused by the nostalgia for their childhoods my mother and her siblings indulge in when together. The stories are inevitably at the expense of one of them. It seems they love each other by putting each other and themselves down.

The dream exposes how much I am and will potentially hurt my mother by healing myself. My grandfather's abuse of his daughters happened in the 1950's. I am fighting that legacy and my fight hurts my mother. The ways my mother has not healed herself are exposed. The ways she has been unable to break this family legacy of abuse herself become apparent. She needs my silence, my acceptance of her version of my childhood, to cope herself with what she has done or not done for me. But I know when I heal, the potential for all our healing is greater. The wounds exposed for my family by my journey have the opportunity to heal.

I sell my truck and trailer. This is great because now I can pay for massage school, but my sadness and sense of loss about my horse resurfaces. Again I have times I cannot stop crying. For whole days I am sad and despairing. And I feel deep shame that I cannot control these emotions. It is exhausting, struggling with myself. Rita suggests I need to grieve. I have no idea how one does this. My grief feels endless. If I let it out unchecked I will never stop crying. My grief for Ross brings up all the losses I never grieved for before this. I have a huge feeling of loss in my life. I usually keep it successfully buried, but any normal adult disappointment or loss triggers this overwhelming emotional response. I feel like an irrational, out-of-control freak. I just want to be a calm adult, dealing with normal adult things with a reasonable range of emotional response.

Diane explains that my extreme emotions are childhood emotions that were not processed at the time. Children are supposed to be irrational and they feel deeply, all the way. That's what parents are for – to comfort the child and model coping. If the parent doesn't know how to cope with emotions, the child never learns. She fends for herself, sometimes coping by stuffing unendurable feelings deep inside. To process and release these feelings the child needs a voice. To grieve she needs to express her sadness. I keep telling my inner little girl to shut up and go away. I am tired of her feelings getting in the way of my adult life. I am tired of being irrational. I cannot function as an adult, go to work, go to the store, if I am in tears all the time. But if I don't start to love this sad little me-girl and treat her differently, nothing will change.

In meditation, *I draw a blue circle around myself large enough for two. I find the grief feeling in my chest. I ask the little girl there if she would like to come into the circle and talk to me. She comes. She wears a yellow cotton dress with small orange flowers on the skirt. We sit next to each other cross-legged. I start the conversation: "How do you feel about Ross?" She says, "It's not fair! Why does Beth get to go to all the shows and ride her horse all the time. Her horse never gets hurt. Everyone else gets to ride everyday, year after year. Why did my horse have to get hurt? It's not fair. Why give me a horse, like I always wanted, and then take it away? What is the point? Ross is broken. I can't ride him anymore. I miss him. I love him but there is nothing to do with him. He doesn't need me while he stands in a field and eats grass. I want to show. I want to jump. I only got to ride Ross for six months. It's not fair!" I hold her on my lap and listen to how she feels. We cry together until we are done.*

I talk to Rita about feeling depressed and overeating. She says I should just go with it. Be depressed. Be as depressed as I can. Eat all the cookie dough I can. She guarantees it won't last, that it is my resistance to the depression that perpetuates it. The resistance itself is self-hate. I tell myself that what I want and what I feel are not okay. "It is wrong to be depressed. It is wrong to give in to these feelings." I don't want to be a depressed or a fat person. The resistance sends hate messages to the parts of myself that need in this moment to be sad. The self-hate messages cause me to need to comfort myself. The need for comfort causes overeating. The overeating causes depression and self-hate. Round and round and round. I see the more I can accept what my body needs in the moment, even if I fear it, the more my body will not need extra, external comfort. With acceptance I will be reinforcing internal safety and comfort.

Rita suggests I actively practice grounding myself. I choose the image of a tree. The trunk, a barrel around my body, leaves me room to move and expand while protecting me from others. The branches reach to the sun, to the sky, to God. The roots dig into the earth. I spread them out from my legs, burrowing into the soil, all the way around in a circle. I carry the image around throughout the day, rebuilding the tree whenever I feel anxious.

Rita's hands work around my solar plexus. The area pooches out. I am extra fat today. As she works I start laughing. I laugh so hard it hurts. I can't breathe. I laugh so hard Rita cannot help but laugh with me. I crack her up. We are in tears and we don't even know what we are laughing about. I giggle the rest of the day. Healing is feeling. It is messy, crazy, chaotic, and unpredictable. But it is real. I know this is me. I am moving into my body, inhabiting parts I have not lived in before. It is terrifying and a great relief. A paradox. Healing is being a whole person, full of conflicting emotions and impulses. It is holding the abuser and the abused, the rapist and the raped, the damaged and the healed, in sympathetic acceptance at the same moment. Laughing and crying seem so close, almost the same feeling.

I dream a small wild grey cat attacks me. *I am in the hayloft of a barn. To get the cat to stop attacking I grab it and stuff it in a dusty hole under the roof. There is a dusty blanket in the hole. I feel bad about stuffing the cat in there. I grab the blanket and pull it out, spinning the cat around in the suffocating dust. The cat runs away. I leave the barn. There is a man waiting to comfort me.*

Since the heart opening session with Sam I feel a renewed sensitivity to animals. I used to feel this way when I was a child. I would get very upset if I saw an animal in pain, even in a movie. In response, my mother would get angry at me, tell me to calm down, tell me there was nothing to get upset about because the movie was not real. I would feel ashamed for feeling so much. In my late teens I shut it off somehow. Now it is back. Once again I cannot handle seeing, even in a story, animals in pain. It hurts too much. Also, my senses feel more acute. As I walk downtown I am overwhelmed by the smells of exhaust, unwashed bodies, urine, and the noise, the traffic too loud. Most surprising of all, I notice I have an open space in my brain, right in the middle, a space clear and quiet even when I am upset, crying, or anxious.

Using my Heart Brain

I dream a Lee-type woman (Lee was a spiritual mentor/mother figure for me in my late twenties) arranges for me to play a flute solo with the symphony. *I do not play the flute, though she does. She gives me the music, called "The Wreck of the Hesperus." Instead of music, pictured on the page is a Rembrandt painting, "Storm on the Sea of Galilee," a ship foundering, men panicking. The flute I am given is very short, just two parts to put together. I practice making noises while the audience arrives. The Lee-woman says it is okay to just fake it – the audience will never know. We're ready to start. I cannot find the right page in the music. I find it but then I cannot get the flute to play. No noise comes out. The orchestra plays behind me but there is no flute melody. Everyone watches. I don't understand how faking it is going to work. I wake having an orgasm.*

The meaning comes to me as I wake. I have been faking it to survive for a long time. The performance anxiety is exhausting. I lived with my mother the majority of the time after the age of two. I was told as a child that the intensity of my love and the power of my feelings was wrong. When I was upset, my mother interpreted my feelings as a threat. It meant she was not a good mother. To survive I had to accept my mother's version of the truth. What I needed and what I felt I had to hide. I had to pretend I wasn't sensitive, passionate, emotional. I had to present a different person to my mother – a calm, non-dependent child. And I had to project confidence in her ability to mother. I had to pretend I felt safe and well-guided even when I didn't.

My anxiety and fatigue as an adult stem from this habit of playing another person who is not me. The faking it is not working anymore. The facade is cracking. In my dream, I cannot get the flute to play even with the music, with instructions, with someone telling me how to be this flute-playing person. Seeing through my own facade, realizing my inability to fake it, creates a release. Energy moves in the orgasm as my true self expands and reveals herself a little bit.

The flute music's title is a poem from Longfellow. A sea captain father takes his daughter to sea "to bear him company." Promising his daughter he can keep her safe, he ignores warnings of a storm:

> "Come hither! come hither! my little daughter,
> And do not tremble so;
> For I can weather the roughest gale
> That ever wind did blow."

> He wrapped her warm in his seaman's coat
> Against the stinging blast;
> He cut a rope from a broken spar,
> And bound her to the mast.

The ship falters in the storm and everyone drowns. The poem ends with a fisherman on the shore finding the daughter's corpse tied to the washed up mast. The biblical story painted by Rembrandt, pictured on the flute score in the dream, is mentioned in the poem. The girl, seeing her father dead, starts praying for salvation, "And she thought of Christ, /Who stilled the wave, /On the Lake of Galilee."

The poem tells of an innocent girl killed by her father's arrogance, of masculine reason and will overpowering the feminine ways of knowing, intuition and feeling. The captain wants his daughter for company, but she is only valued for her surface (she is lovely to look at) not her whole person (what she can sense or her voice):

> Blue were her eyes as the fairy flax,
> Her cheeks like the dawn of day,
> And her bosom white as the hawthorn buds,
> That ope in the month of May.

As a daughter on her father's ship, she has no choice but to trust him to survive, and he believes he can best the sea, that he is stronger than nature. The captain dismisses the things his daughter senses, not considering the possibility that what she hears and sees could help. As the ship founders in the gale, the girl hears church bells and then gunshots from another ship, two possible directions to safety. Then she sees a "gleaming light," but her father has already drowned:

> "O father! I hear the church bells ring,
> Oh, say, what may it be?"
> "Tis a fog-bell on a rock bound coast!" –
> And he steered for the open sea.
>
> "O father! I hear the sound of guns;
> Oh, say, what may it be?"
> Some ship in distress, that cannot live
> In such an angry sea!"
>
> "O father! I see a gleaming light.

Oh say, what may it be?"
But the father answered never a word,
A frozen corpse was he.

The church bells could be a safe harbor or the salvation of God. The gunshots could be another ship trying to signal a rescue. All her father senses is danger, no safe harbor but rocky shore, no rescue ship but a weaker vessel. His inability to trust or allow other ways of knowing dooms the ship. Tied to the mast, a phallic representation of her father's will, the daughter has to accept his world-view. He dies for his hubris and takes her with him. She eventually sees the light, but has accepted her father's world-view so completely, she needs him to interpret the light's meaning. With him dead, she prays, but it is too late.

It is an old story, humans and their minds believing they can outwit nature, take on Zeus. The poem can be interpreted as a warning, not only about human arrogance, but also about the imbalance of privileging masculine ways of knowing, the left-brain, reason-is-God ways, over feminine, right-brain, intuition and feeling ways of knowing. As Caroline Myss explains in *Sacred Contracts*, when your heart and mind do not work together, each becomes fixed and over-emphasized in their separate roles. The heart becomes too emotional, the mind too rational, and the person becomes dominated by this conflict of opposing forces and the fear such inner-conflict engenders.

Within such an imbalance, reason becomes blind will, untempered by intuition from experience and feeling. My parents were over-educated. My mother has a PhD in genetics. She worked her way up to the top in a consumer products company. My father had a PhD in microbiology, and an MD. He worked as a psychiatrist. Both sought in early adulthood, to varying success, a left-brain, scientific answer to life's problems to avoid their own emotional problems and difficult childhoods. This world-view, forced upon me by my mother's insecurity, did not work well for me as a child. There was no space for a sensitive, emotional, large-hearted child.

A few days after the flute dream, I find an article in the New York Times Magazine by Amy Fusselman. She writes about her frustration with years of talk therapy and being tired of using only her brain to solve problems. She describes trying alternative treatments like energy healing bodywork, and the relief she feels with this more heart and body based approach. I am also done being tied to the mast. I don't believe my left-brain has all the answers anymore. That side is strong and useful for many things in life, but not all things. To play the flute I would have to learn with my body. My lips and lungs would have to practice and figure it out. My brain can't help all that much. I am ready for a new way of learning, a body way. I can still use my brain, but I want to use it appropriately. Relax the brain's God complex. Make a little room for other ways of knowing.

I complain to Rita about this fear I carry around all the time. She asks where it is. *On the table I locate the fear in my chest – a long knife across my heart up to my right eye. I pull the knife out. There is a deep slash left in my chest over my heart. Rita suggests I have my left-brain come take a look at the problem and this man in a lab coat shows up lickety-split, clutching a clipboard. He peers at the hole in my chest from behind his glasses, curious and worried. He takes all sorts of measurements, making notes. I crack up laughing. He is so intent and serious, so Mr. Scientist. He doesn't know what to do but he collects lots of data.*

I invite my right brain to have a go. A flowing, longhaired and skirted woman dances over in purple and blue. She smiles, serene, present, grounded, unworried and unhurried. She gives Mr. Left Brain a job to go measure the other end of the hole. When he is occupied elsewhere, she asks the wound what it needs. She lies down in the wound. She is the wound. She sews up the ends as far as possible then allows the middle to slowly fill in. I feel a strong, hot pulse in the area of the hole. Mr. Left Brain says, "How interesting, that's the same phenomenon we read about in that craniosacral book!" He takes more notes.

Something to Give Back

As Rita moves from craniosacral therapist to spiritual mentor and friend, my husband balks at meeting her. He doesn't want her in our house. He doesn't trust her. He thinks she has poor boundaries and too much power over me. I don't know. I have a pattern of abandoning myself to teachers in this way. He thinks it is wrong for me to be as vulnerable to Diane and Rita as I am, that having weak boundaries with teachers or parent figures it is a learned response to incest. I think that vulnerability is how I learn and grow. I don't know another way to do it – to radically change my world-view to open to God. He feels what incest taught me must be entirely unlearned. I think it is a gift – a gift of openness, vulnerability, defenselessness. My path feels right and good. I feel guided to want to learn craniosacral therapy. My husband does not understand having a path. He feels my way is dangerous. And it is – it is dangerous to change and transform, to risk my own mistakes.

Our disagreement leaves me confused and upset. I don't want to lose my husband over this. I wonder if learning/growing and giving my power away to people are two different things I experience at the same time. Perhaps I don't have to do both. Maybe I don't have to give my power away to a person to learn. But how do I find the difference between giving my power away to a mentor and surrendering to divine guidance?

One of the first classes I take at massage school is Communications. After class one night, I ask my teacher for help. I am in tears. He has me sit down for a minute on the floor facing him. He tells me to feel into my desire to learn craniosacral therapy, to locate where I feel it in my body. He asks me to move my body to be in that feeling. I lean a little to the right, curling slightly over my rib cage. He prompts me to look at where I feel my husband's view, at our disconnection, our argument. I look to the left. I feel relieved and less tearful as I look this way. I feel less lost and confused. Less despairing. I realize this teacher has given me an experience of staying in my own power while considering another person's view. I never learned to do this with people I need or care about. I learned as a child to accept my parent's point of view so completely that I cannot remember my own when faced with the other's. Maybe I need not abandon my own point of view, what feels true to me, to consider another's perspective.

That weekend I get to practice what I have learned. I take the Shambhala Buddhism Level I course at the meditation center. The teacher happens to have terminal cancer. I have high expectations of seeing a teacher who is able to teach us about death, about how to die, about acceptance, detachment, love. This is perhaps an unfair expectation for a lay Shambhala teacher. I am disappointed. He seems bitter and angry in his talks, unable to project a sense of peace or acceptance. This is understandable for anyone facing death, but it is not inspiring in a teacher. He teaches about "basic goodness" but then warns us not to be lazy, that we have to try harder to be good.

To make it through the course, I use the image of the tree to feel grounded and impermeable to other's thoughts and opinions I do not wish to take inside. When I do not agree with what the teacher says, rather than convince myself something is wrong with me, I practice letting his feelings and his view be his. I do not let them seep into me. I do not want his negative feelings. I don't believe in laziness. There is a reason when people are lethargic, locked in place, and shaming them does nothing to reach the real issue.

I practice taking what I find helpful from the weekend and letting the rest go. I feel powerful and grateful, more present and confident in such a group activity than I have before. I realize the teacher has shown us how to be a frightened and bitter human being. I feel empathy for his situation, but this is not the lesson I am seeking from a teacher. I wish to be inspired to grow spiritually, not to leave my humanness, but to manage it more gracefully.

When I get home from the course, my husband reminds me what an amazing person he is. Talking out my dissonance with the Level I program opens communication between us again. Our anger and fear have settled down. We reiterate our original understanding, from before we married, of our different spiritual paths. We simply believe what works for each of us. We each choose to see the world in a way that makes our lives what we want, but they are all just beliefs, ways we choose to interpret our existence in the world. He chooses to see the world as finite, material, what you see is what you get. He does not believe there is a master plan to our existence or hidden forces influencing our lives. I choose to believe I am guided, that God exists and there is some master plan that we are too limited to comprehend. I feel the truth of this and I choose to believe in that feeling. Each of us thinks the other is mistaken but this does not mean we cannot love each other and be partners. Being introverts, it is a miracle we mated at all. We both need a lot of room to feel comfortable. I know if my husband was going through similar spiritual growth right next to me I would feel crowded and unable to differentiate my own experiences. It helps me to bounce my experiences off his skeptical viewpoint. I learn to stand on my own feet, to validate my own perspective.

He admits his that his aversion to meeting Rita is instinctual, not logical, and this bothers him. I respect this. After all, I am trying to listen to my own instincts and intuition more, to follow what feels right for me. He tells me he understands why I might feel insecure right now, like everything is changing and I don't know who I am. I have been defining myself as an Eventer, my life has been all about horses. Losing that identity, though an opportunity, is painful, frightening. He's gone through the same sort of identity shift around music and touring in bands. I remember the love my husband and I share. We like to talk to each other, to work things out. We both think deeply about our lives and what we want them to be. We want to be decent, high integrity human beings. He tells me that what I have gone through in the last year is not what he would have preferred, but he sees he is growing as a human being in ways he would not have without the prod of his commitment to me, and while that is difficult, he is grateful.

I use the image of a plumb line bisecting my body when I feel off center or confused. I put the line back in the middle and feel into that place to find my grounding and be clear. I work on letting go of doubt. I tell Sam about my father and the sexual abuse. During the session, he takes my jaw in both his hands, his thumbs in my mouth resting on my molars, and tells me to resist him with my whole body. We wrestle this way for a while. I sense I am supposed to feel angry in my jaw, that this is what Sam expects, that I did not get to fight back and this needs to be expressed, but this does not feel true to me.

I go back to the center of me with my plumb line and find what feels true. I was a baby. My jaw did bite down. It is not anger I feel in the strength of my jaw clenching but a drive to suckle, to seek comfort. While I accept this as the truth, I feel ashamed. I can't tell Sam this. At a later point in the session, after the jaw work, I cough deeply several times. Sam asks me to cover my mouth when I cough. I feel instantly unsafe and again ashamed. I know at that moment I will not come back for more sessions with Sam.

This is okay. I learn something. Needing his clients to cover their mouths when they cough is simply Sam's boundary. He is right to state it. This is not the kind of boundary I will have in my bodywork practice. On the table I feel like a child. I am working out child feelings, having child coughs. Children do not cover their mouths. Acting like a child in my body is the release, the healing. It is necessary. Allowing my clients to do what they need to on the table is important to me. I am willing to expose myself to their germs in order for them to have this opportunity to heal.

I begin to have moments of well-being, of feeling entirely well, home, clear and relaxed. I think, "I am finally the person I have always wanted to be." I love massage school. My class goes to a retreat center for a weekend to practice massage on the public. Staying an entire three days in the company of other people usually takes my anxiety through the roof. Amazingly though, I am fine. To my surprise and pleasure, I enjoy the time with my classmates. I find them beautiful and interesting. My energy is not so entangled with my own emotional problems. I have room to be curious about and present with other people. This is no less than a miracle.

I am learning that to touch and feel is to experience life, to become one with life. I feel confident; able to be present in such a way that I can accept whatever feelings I have in the moment and deal with the situation. Back in town, waiting at a bus stop, I experience my mind as quiet, open, at rest. For a moment I am a mirror – my stillness simply reflecting the street, the light, the cars, the people. For a week everything looks brighter in color. I notice details, the shape of the trees, the baby spring leaves, bubbles in puddles. Walking downtown one stormy day I have a conversation with a cloud. Dark grey, ready to pour, I say, "You'd better not! Just give me 10 minutes!" I have fun.

On May 1st, invited to share my experience as a member of the community, I give a talk at the Buddhist center. It makes me nervous but I can do public speaking.

Before the talk, during the group meditation, I build my grounding tree. I expand my heart out to touch everyone in the room. I find I am not afraid of them. I feel connected to them and secure myself. I am willing to stumble in public if I need to. Trusting myself means I am allowed to learn and make mistakes. I tell them:

Today is May 1st – May Day in the Irish tradition is Beltane. To celebrate they would build huge fires and dance through the smoke for purification. This would clear the body of evil spirits and the stagnation of winter to make way for spring and new life. I often feel possessed by evil spirits. No really, have you ever had a thought or emotion that just wouldn't go away? Like when someone cuts you off on the freeway and then *they* give *you* the finger. I can stew about the absolute injustice of that for days, and nights. So now this inconsiderate stranger is robbing me of sleep but the other driver is not actually in my bed, it is me alone, making *myself* angry.

I think the worst of my evil sprits are deeply ingrained habits of mind that trap me in doubt and fear. I have lived with disabling anxiety most of my life. At times I would have trouble leaving the house just to go to the grocery store – a place I've been a thousand times without incident. I think this is the worst part – that the fear doesn't make sense, so I'm ashamed of it. At its worst I fully convince myself that my husband will leave me before I figure it all out. I believe there is something fundamentally wrong with me, something that I have to fix before I am lovable – before I am worthy of my husband's love.

For me one of the greatest gifts of meditation has been the power to choose what to believe from what I think. The evil spirit thoughts control my life less because I just don't believe them as easily anymore. I have sat with them, examined them, and found them to be untrustworthy. To my wonder and eternal gratitude, I have found a more fundamental existence underneath them. I realize when I sit with myself, I am worthy of love just how I am – there is nothing to fix. I am whole already, and I have been given all the tools I need, including my anxiety, with which to find my true self. Now I see the fear as a gift – my anxiety drove me to search further, to get to know myself more deeply.

I think the experience I found in meditation is what Chogyam Trungpa calls basic goodness. I understand that my basic nature is good. Underneath all the fear of not being enough and the compulsion for self-improvement, I realize I am ordinary and good at the core. I can relax here, no remodeling needed.

I close the talk by reading Mary Oliver's *The Wild Geese*. I feel so comforted by this poem and the idea that we do not have to try to be good. We just need to allow the love in our core nature to move us. Several people thank me for speaking, moved by my openness and vulnerability. It feels wonderful. I have something to give back.

Something Called Blue Fire

Rita talks to Osho and other spirit-realm guides. She often refers to "They" – "They say" – as if she is getting information in real time and relaying it to me. I have kind of ignored this so far. I don't know if it is real or possible, if spirit-type things exist. I am attracted to the idea, yet afraid of the paradigm shift required to go there. It seems to me there is only God and us embodied folk. I feel guided by God. I try to intuit how to go forward and trust the feeling. I experience the mystery of asking for help and receiving an answer through the Osho Cards, but I don't feel like that comes from a guide personal to me, some spiritual entity following me around.

I specifically do not wish to contact Osho directly, even if that is possible. I am afraid of him. He is mixed up with my feelings about my father. Rita mentions she is going to do something called "Blue Fire." The name captures my attention. She explains Blue Fire is about getting help with your stuff. "They" will actually come down and clean house for you so you don't have to do all this work sorting through your own baggage. That sounds good to me. I make an appointment with Anna, a facilitator for Blue Fire. I guess I am ready to cross the line.

During my first session with Anna I specifically do not ask what Blue Fire is or anything about "They." I just go with my desire to do Blue Fire and see for myself what happens. I want to know from my own experience what this is all about. I don't want anyone else to tell me. She asks if I have a female spirit guide. I have no idea. She says the guide might be sort of like Athena, the Greek goddess who sprang from the head of Zeus. I don't know what to make of this but I'm game. I receive instructions for two meditations, one to meet this guide, the other to comfort my little girl. She cautions me to go slowly when I do these exercises, to walk the journey as if I were walking with my feet in my body, in real time, to feel the experience.

I buy a set of Medicine Cards. I randomly pick **Owl**. Interestingly, the explanation of the card mentions Athena. The Greek Goddess has and owl on her shoulder to enable her to see into the dark and to know the whole truth. Sitting in meditation, I visit my little girl. *I ask to be shown a door. It is green with a brass knob. I walk carefully through the door and down the stairs on the other side. The stairs have a plush green carpet, a wooden banister. Another door is at the bottom, white with a crystal knob. I emerge in a field of tall grass, a hillside meadow. It is windy, sunny and warm. I can see the ocean, a beach below. I ask my little girl if she wants to come meet me here. She comes.*

She has a white cotton dress on over jeans. She is barefoot. Her hair is long, white-blond. We roll in the grass. Swing on a swing set. I ask if she wants a house here. She says she doesn't need one. I ask what she needs. She says she doesn't want to be left alone. I fear for a moment that I cannot give her what she wants. I cannot stay here with her. Then I realize where we are – we are inside me. I explain that we are in my heart, that this entire safe, fun, free world for her exists in me. She is not alone; she is always with me. She can play with me anytime. I go back through the door, up the stairs to home. I feel some resolution here but there is still work to be done. She still hates being left alone. She doesn't entirely trust me, and for good reason as I still resent having to take care of her.

Another day that week I do the other meditation: *I picture an elevator, a large silver sliding door, wood panels on the inside. I walk into the elevator and turn around. I press a button and ask to be taken up a few levels to one that is clear and neutral. The elevator rises and then stops. The door opens. I walk out into white space. I picture two chairs and sit down in one. I ask Athena if she would like to come meet me. I offer her the other chair. She appears as a gold energy egg shape the size of my torso. She radiates gold light. She doesn't need the chair. I invite her closer and I feel her in front of my body, crossing into my body lightly, just a few inches. I ask, "How can I nurture this relationship?" I hear, "Open to it." I ask, "How close can I be to you all the time?" I hear, "As close as you wish, as you can tolerate and feel comfortable." I ask, "What should I call you?" I hear, "Athena is fine." I feel like crying but no tears come. I thank her and say good-bye. I come back home in the elevator, full of energy.*

I ask my husband if I can take over our yoga room for my Blue Fire work. The room is painted blue. We already call it the "blue room." I need a safe place just for me to explore on my own. He is upset about this, even though he has a whole corner of the basement to himself, for his computer and his music. He agrees reluctantly and again I feel afraid for us, that I am moving further away from him and our marriage.

I dream I have an affair in the same house my husband and I share. *I spend the day with this other man. I love being held by him, it feels fully complete, encompassing, safe, comforting. I want to be with him more. He broke out of jail on his own. Because he is so free, I cannot be with him like in a marriage, like I have in this life. I feel terrible guilt about betraying my husband. I plan to lie about where I have been all day but I don't want to lie.*

I wake and realize this dream is about Blue Fire and "crossing the line." I am now "talking" to spirit guides. I worry about whether to tell my husband about it or not. I feel like I am betraying him. I don't want to keep it a secret. I decide to simply use other words if we talk about it. Rather than, "Blue Fire is helping me find my spirit guides," I'll say, "Blue Fire helps me get in touch with my intuition." Mostly, we don't talk about it.

My friend Ellen, in conversation, calls me "a lady of leisure." I am in school and not working right now. I spend my time and energy on healing. To the outside world, it doesn't look like I do much. She wishes she had my life, a husband, house, security. What she says bothers me a lot. I struggle not to feel guilty for what I have, not to feel useless or ashamed for doing internal work. I try putting her words in an envelope and mailing them back to her but they persist in my head. Rita suggests responding with gratitude. Deflect the judgment with something like "Yeah, my life is great. I am grateful for what I have." But once again I wonder how to defend myself against other people's judgments and opinions. I still let them sink in and hurt me, I doubt myself or feel there is something wrong with me and my life.

Ellen thinks she is ripped off, that she doesn't have what she deserves to have at her age. Rita explains that you can look at a person's attitude as their particular hole. Ellen is down in her hole, digging it deeper with envy and resentment. Rita says you don't go down into the hole with them. Just kneel on the edge. Reflect back to them what you hear they are feeling and meaning. People have to be heard and feel heard before they can find a way out of their hole. Anna suggests I keep the entire conversation in a basket between me and the other person. What I say, what they say, all goes in the basket. Not into me. When the talking is over, each person can take what she needs from the basket and the rest can be composted.

I receive an email from my former trainer, a woman I now realize I gave complete control to regarding my horse. I am slowly seeing I don't want anyone controlling my life anymore. I am no longer looking for a mother. Ross lives at another farm now. He has good days and bad days, sometimes sore and sometimes fine. My trainer happened to be at this farm recently and saw him on a bad day. She emails to urge me to take him to the vet for more tests and opinions or to put him down. After two years of (expensive) tests and opinions, I have had enough. I know Ross is fine, not suffering, but her email throws me into a well of guilt and doubt again.

In this frightened and painful headspace, I decide to try something new, something kind of crazy. I sit down in meditation and reach out to Ross. I picture what he looks like, what he is doing. I see him in the field, shaking his head, butting his buddy. I ask him if his leg hurts. If I should do something more for him, follow my trainer's advice further. I clearly hear, "Don't listen to her." I have to trust myself. I don't know if I am doing the right thing for Ross but I have to trust my own instincts now, take responsibility for my own decisions. I pull **Badger** from the Medicine Cards. The card tells me to be fierce about separating myself from old connections that block my healing.

Now that our anger has lessened, my mother and I exchange emails. I see that we will never agree about what happened when I left her in the hospital. I feel ready to see her. I go for a visit around Mother's Day. We both seem relieved to have reestablished contact. We avoid talking about anything upsetting. I hope to be able to visit her when I can do it with an open heart, when I am not angry or resentful, or processing too much about my own childhood to be available to her. This means I limit how much time I spend with her. This will not make her happy, but as long as she doesn't push this boundary, we will be able to have some contact.

Free Associating

Anna asks me about animal spirit guides. I show her the tribal tattoo of a jumping horse on my right leg. I tell her about the dream with the black panther. I start to see Horse and Panther as guides. In the dream, I worried about how brutal I was with the panther – now I see the fight as a struggle with my fears. In the Medicine Cards, **Black Panther** is about the courage to move forward into what is yet unknown, to face fear and to look into the dark for healing. The card also mentions finding the strength and patience to tolerate mystery.

In the dream the father-man says the cat is a threat, and that we have to protect ourselves by standing on the picnic tables. This is his meaning, his interpretation of events. I feel whole, beautiful, perfect as I am – this is new for me. I feel no shame that the father-man has called me fat. I am no longer playing by known rules. I was told to fear the cat but the way I was told to protect myself did not work, and I had to hurt the most pure, beautiful thing in the dream – the panther. What if I had embraced the cat's coming without fear?

Rita lends me *Daughters of Copper Woman* by Anne Cameron. I am struck by a passage where Copper Woman, alone and in despair, begins to cry such that a large wad of mucous falls from her nose. Ashamed, she tries to cover it up with sand until some magic women tell her to stop, that the snot is to be cherished. They explain that if she can learn to accept her feelings, she will never be lonely.

I am ashamed of my grief. It spills over like a big wad of mucous for all to see. I try to hide it but I feel like crying a lot of the time. My sense of separation makes me lonely. If my suffering and grief are my very own, my unique personal cross to bear, then I am indeed alone. And I am creating my loneliness by seeing my suffering as separate from other humans. If I thank my grief for teaching me, for serving me, I join with my legacy as a human being, with other human beings in grief and loss. I am not alone. We all share in our vulnerability and mortality.

I dream I go to the grave of a Native American elder murdered years ago. *His people have performed a ritual there every year in the hope that the dead man would reveal who killed him. The elder has never answered. For the ritual, we kneel on the floorboards. There are cracks between them, a space underneath the floor. A huge mayfly crawls out from between the boards. I shove it away from me and it goes behind me. The mayfly eats a huge hairy spider, chewing off one leg at a time.*

In my second session with Anna I cry a lot. When I talk to her I cannot piece together a coherent, linear story. I end up free-associating, just going with whatever I need to say. Walking home, I feel overwhelmed, exhausted. I go to bed. I sleep the whole afternoon. My homework is to talk to the four directions. Once again, I don't know what this means but I am willing to try. This exercise has to do with creating sacred space for this work. To practice what the directions feel like, get to know them a little, try to balance the energy in the room.

A few days later I try it. In meditation I sit facing South, spending time with each direction and gathering my impressions. *In the South I see desert and the fire of the sun, heat, red. In the North I see a mountain, cold, white/blue ice. In the East I see birth, beginnings, pink. In the West, dark smoke, time passing, death. I sense that I, in the middle, am the key to balancing the energies. My body already balances hot and cold, South and North. I feel a strong energetic flow from the East out the window to the West. I try to halt it in the center, within me, but this doesn't work well.*

Anna suggests grounding my impressions with objects or pictures of them, in an altar or placed around the room. She mentions placing something in the window that will curve the energy going West down toward the ground to create a circle. The energy from East to West can then circle through the Earth. I sense this will ground, cleanse, and conserve the energy. I go to the rock store and find an orange fire-shaped rock for South, a blue ice-crystal rock for North. In the East I place a piece of rose quartz, for birth and love. In the West window I hang a clear crystal-cut sphere. I enjoy making this little space. I have fun with it, placing the rocks where it feels right.

In our third session I talk about self-doubt, about the right thing to do for Ross, about craniosacral therapy and whether I can support myself doing this obscure bodywork. Anna says to take doubt words out of my vocabulary. Make the decision not to doubt and consciously discard thoughts that send me into insecurity. During the session I feel myself "downloading," taking in energetic information. Like something is opening the center of my head and vibrating my limbic system and pituitary gland. She gives me a specific assignment from Athena. I am to write a story about Athena as a "mythical powered being" and make a collage of my "future self." I am to travel to a body of water and talk to the earth, the water, a sacred object, and an animal. I see right away I am to go to my favorite beach on the coast. As I walk home, I see Athena in Zeus' head, like a headache.

I start the story and get stuck. The Critic comes in and shuts me down. I get my period, a migraine, and nose-dive into negative thinking. I doubt the meditations I've done. I feel intensely insecure. I fear I'm making it all up, that none of this is real. I decide what my "future self" collage will look like. I think of a certain picture I want but cannot find it in the magazines. My ideas are not good enough. I sit and stare at the table for a long time, getting nowhere. Finally, after several tries, I give up and do something new. I start pulling out pictures that I like even if I don't know why I like them or what picture I am making. I find the pictures making the collage. They naturally go together. It turns out perfectly, full of the ancient and new, mystery, beauty, strength, possibility.

I have this space in my head now that is always open and quiet. The space is there even when I am upset, even when something has triggered my emotions. I sense if I can release or quiet my resistance to being upset or emotional, I can be fine and upset at the same time. The quiet peace in my head is constant. The upset emotions are temporary. I can trust this. Now that I know I am deeply okay even when I feel upset, I can float through it, ride it out. I will be fine on the other side. I can be patient now. Take it all more lightly. I have lived through these emotional triggers so many times I know it will pass. Thoughts become just another event, like the rain or sun, Monday or Saturday. My mind and my personality take their place within my whole being – they are no longer the main show.

I begin to experience space between me and other people. I have little or no emotional response, like I used to, to other people's stories and dramas. I start to see the hurtful words and actions of others as stemming from their upset mind, from being triggered. The people doing the hurt are in pain themselves. They are just taking care of what they think they need, doing their best in the moment to get out of pain. This does not mean I have to participate. I can get out of the way of the tornado. I do not need to witness their personal drama. I can be unavailable.

I practice getting into the direct sensory experience of just being when I feel upset or triggered. I switch my attention from reacting to and rejecting my emotional pain to something right in front of me. I can be sad, crying, and in that moment also carefully wash a white dinner plate, feel my foot push me across the rain soaked sidewalk, run my fingers over my cat's luscious brown and gold back. I find confidence comes from being grounded in the present moment, no matter my mind's turmoil or the world's business around me. Confidence comes from accepting, living fully in, my entire self, all my seemingly conflicting parts, the emotional pain and the underlying peace, in the same moment. I can stop creating cover stories to present to the world to hide how I really am. I am too exhausted to do this pretending anyway. I sense it may be a hell of a lot easier to live my existence as is, exposed warts and tears and all.

Talking to Whales

I have always done art or writing as a task to complete. I get it done as soon as possible. I find I am now taking my time. The process becomes about discovery rather than task completion. Inspiration will come if I make space for it. Before I work on the Athena story again, I check in with my little girl: *I go down the stairs and through the door. She greets me happily in the sunny, breezy meadow, the tall grass waving around. There is a schoolhouse there now. This feels safe. I love school. I know what to expect. I learn easily in this structured environment and soak up the praise. The adults are there to help me. I can trust them. They are generally kind and behave predictably. My little girl takes me down to the beach. We dance together in the water. She is full of energy and free. When I leave she is without fear or resentment. She is happy and light.*

I finish the Athena story:

Athena, a Mythical Powered Being

She started as a thought in his head and She'd been there, in his right frontal lobe, through most of his existence. When he drank, the edges of Her being floated apart and forgot which thought they belonged to. When he was bored, She was restless. When he was depressed, She felt heavy like a thick unliftable fog. When he chased wood nymphs down by the river, She felt his excitement, his lust, churning below Her. Sometimes he would hear a desperate plea from one of the hapless mortals who lived out their short lives tied to the earth below. At these times She felt useful, urging him to intervene, to make a difference. And sometimes he listened to Her. Folks said he was the most powerful of gods, that he ruled the heavens. But he wasn't happy addicted to his next bolt of lightning. She never had any peace. His thoughts galloped around Her endlessly like a herd of wild horses. And She was tired of the pounding hooves, the dust, the endless rush.

It was the Leda episode that did it – finally pushed Her to find a way out. The whole thing was so confusing, the wash of his emotions overwhelming. First there was the chase, the old excitement, the lust pounding through his mind and body, the poor girl at once trying to please the god and terrified of what he wanted. Stuck in his head, drunk on his desire, She wanted to fuck the girl, too, and She didn't even have a body of Her own to fuck with. Then came the inkling of guilt (he was married after all) and his wife was not a god to cross lightly. She was pricked by his tiny pang of regret as he remembered his last conquest turned into a cow.

He paused the chase for Leda in a sheltered meadow that sloped down to a lake. He let the terrified girl catch her breath, her hands clasped over her breasts, her gown long lost to the chase, while he pondered the wife problem, going over the pros and cons. She was trying to emphasize the cons in his head as he rested on a stone bench, looking over the lake, his heated body ready as ever, but he wasn't paying attention. He just needed to hide the deed to get away with it. He saw a lone swan across the lake, magnificent in its pristine white down, idly riding the currents stirred up in the summer breeze. He looked back to the girl, curled in the grass, her eyes a trapped doe's, and with a thought hid his godly form in the body of a swan. He came at Leda then, confident in his disguise, the giant bird tearing into her shoulder to hold her down while he forced his body into hers. When the haze of lust cleared his mind, he looked down at the girl's belly and thighs, covered with bloody white feathers, and felt ashamed.

None of this was new, the raping, the remorse, but She was starting to realize that the excitement, lust, shame, and regret weren't hers. They were a part of her because She was a part of him, but She had learned them here, in his head, and She could unlearn them. It was his deception that gave her the idea. If he could take a different form with a thought, and She was a thought, why couldn't She? So She imagined what She must look like. She was female, that was a given, a big woman, strong and powerful, muscular and soft. And She was angry after all these years stuck in his head, trapped in his world, swimming in his emotions, beaten down by his thoughts. That anger was her strength. She realized all She had endured and yet survived. She was a fighter, a warrior.

Suddenly there wasn't enough room in his head for the both of them. Luckily She was wearing armor, with a helmet, because her head, now come into being, was pushed up hard against the inside of his skull. Her arms jutted from his frontal cortex to his cerebellum and her legs stretched down his spine, her feet scrunched into his pelvis. She poked around with her spear, looking for a way out, and noticed the movement of his cranial bones. The sutures widened and narrowed in rhythm, and She squeezed through at their widest point, cutting her way out through the thick tissue with her spear. She sprung from his head fully armed, vowing to live from that day forward fully on her own, in her own body, guided by her own wisdom.

To finish my homework from Anna, I drive to my favorite state park on the coast. I hike up the trail to a salal-hidden spot on a cliff overlooking an isolated rocky beach. It is a lovely, sunny and cool spring day. I tune into the Ocean: *Tears, saline, salt water, sad, sure, can hold all the tears, safe, knowing, womb of the earth, amniotic fluid, nourishing, generates life, in my body I have an ocean, saline in my vessels and cells, I carry the ocean, she nourishes me, she moves within me, waves rolling through my fluid body, change, violent movement, power, breaking rock, depth, stillness, vast quiet deep, dark, sunlight sparkles, whales.*

The whales slowly swim together up and down near the surface. The larger Whale tells me his story: *I have traveled this way many times. I have a mate with me. I have lived long alone. When I look for food I travel long alone. This is the way of being whale. I meet others. We travel the coast together. I have a long wound on my back that I have healed. My mate is young and not wounded. This is the way of being whale.*

I take off my hiking boots and press my toes into the wet dirt of the cliff. I tune into the Earth: *Roots, home, core alive, gravity required for life, what we hold on to, dull matter, potential for life, medium for life, heart of fire, movement over millennia, slower than slow, orientation, context, meaning, duality, contrast, direction, container, manifestation.*

Sitting there, I realize I have forgotten how much I like to just be outside, without agenda or direction. All of my outside activity for the last several years has been with horses. It sounds like the perfect way to be with nature except, ironically, I was never present in that way. I was always striving to be a better rider, to have my horse in better condition. I rarely looked around and took a deep breath. The Ocean from this viewpoint is incredible, deep blue-green near the shore, sparkling navy out to sea, one undulating mass. I am so high I can see the curve of the Earth. I love to hike, climb, be with the trees and grasses. I feel strong and free.

Down on the beach, climbing over the boulders between beaches, I find a large volcanic rock. It is lighter than it should be for its size. This makes the sense of gravity when I lift it, the rock's connection to the Earth, more apparent somehow. This rock came from the heart of the Earth, the molten core. It was made in fire. The memory of its birth lives in its connection to the core of the Earth, the weight of it, the resistance to being lifted. This connection exists no matter where the rock rests. This connection exists when I take the rock home and place it in my blue room. My husband calls him "Iggy," for he is an igneous rock. I place him under "Bling," the crystal hanging in the western window of the room. The gravity-fed tension between them is lovely.

Everything Included

Anna reads me the famous Marianne Williamson quote ("Our Deepest Fear...) about how we are actually afraid of our own power. If we let ourselves fully be ourselves, wholly as we are without hiding parts in shame, then we give others permission to do the same. I find am already guided. My feelings for things, my innate inclinations, already speak to and seek to be in tune with my surroundings, other beings, and the Earth around me. All I need do is trust myself, be who I already am without shrinking from it, judging it, or otherwise getting in the way.

Anna gives me four "Gates of Consciousness" to work on for two weeks. In closing the gates, I isolate and defeat myself. In keeping them open, I create possibility and change. The gate closed is the negative statement; the gate open is the positive one:

1) I'm not enough. / I am enough.
2) There is no infinite. / God exists.
3) You (the other is) are not enough. / You (other) are enough.
4) This is too much work, I'm overwhelmed. / This is effortless.

Anna asks me to notice what it feels like when the gates close versus when they are open. Over the next week, I realize I am being asked to practice believing in abundance. Not only in external, practical, material things, like enough food, money, or work, but also in internal, intangible things like my inner attitude, whether I am enough for the situation. I notice how often I tell myself I am not good enough, how I create my own insecurity with a negative internal dialogue. I discover that I tell myself I am not enough most of the time.

That week I pull **Rabbit** from the Medicine Cards three different times, once even after putting it back and trying again. The card is called "Fear" and I don't like it. The story goes: *Rabbit and Witch are best friends. The Witch* *uses her magic to care for Rabbit, conjuring him a turnip when he is hungry and some water when he is thirsty. She even heals him when he falls down a cliff. After the healing, he begins to avoid her. When she finally finds him and confronts him, he tells her he doesn't want anything to do with her magic. Hurt and disappointed, Witch curses him. From then on, whatever Rabbit fears, he will call to him. When he fears Eagle, he will yell for Eagle to not eat him and if Eagle doesn't hear him, he will yell louder till Eagle hears him and swoops down to carry him off.*

In the past, I have felt shame when I get this card, as if something I keep hidden inside is suddenly visible. The fact I am secretly afraid, that deep down, I base my life decisions on fear, is exposed. The card has felt like an admonishment. In the light of the Gates, I understand the card in a different way. If I am enough *as I am* in this moment, if God exists, if Mother Earth is enough, then there is an abundance of safety. If I cling to my fears, let them rule me to such an extent that I might as well be shouting them to the world, then I am rejecting God's love and abundance. If I choose fear as my primary life guide, I am rejecting God's guidance. If I admit, acknowledge, God's abundance, wisdom and guidance in my life, if I choose to benefit from such a view, then it is rude to continue hobbling through life leaning on my crutch of fear.

I need to walk forward on my own two feet, try something new.

Right after these revelations I face a test. Playing a relaxed game of catch with my husband I lean over to pick up the ball and my *sacroiliac* joint goes out. For a moment I cannot stand up. Eventually I can walk gingerly home with my pelvis tucked under. My entire lower back has frozen in place. Any movement I make must be done very carefully as the back is pretty much attached to everything. I cannot do much without pulling on the injured area and eliciting severe pain. This seems supremely unfair. I am only thirty-seven years old. I cannot even go outside and play a game of catch without my body giving out. I feel old, defeated.

I ask Rita for an emergency session. I cry a lot and laugh. While she works on my hip I see my *psoas* muscle on the right side holding a lot of anger. The muscle cannot do its regular job of supporting my torso because it has done this holding work for so long. Rita suggests that these back pain episodes could be releases rather than new injuries, weaknesses, or something wrong with me. This is another one of those moments when the most amazing insight comes out of her mouth. It turns my whole mental situation around.

I think back to the other two times my lower back has gone out. The first time I bent over to put a cat down that I had been holding and found I could not stand up again. In the months before that moment I had gotten married, moved to a new house, quit a stressful nursing job, and started Zoloft for my anxiety. It was a time when suddenly a lot of stresses were over and I could relax. The second time I was at the chiropractor. I remember specifically asking my back to relax while she adjusted me. I wanted to be a "good" patient and she had expressed that she wished that adjustment would go further. Well, it worked, my back slipped right out of joint.

I see Rita is right. These are releases. These moments of relaxation create the conditions for my body to stop holding something, to release an old stuck area. This time, with the Gates, I am working on changing an entire world-view from fear and scarcity to love and abundance. With this opening I create the conditions for yet another release from my *psoas* muscles and *sacroiliac* joint. As I let go of old beliefs and thought patterns, they come out of my body.

A few days later, still uncomfortable, I ask Rita for another session. She is busy but she suggests I try doing craniosacral work on myself. This challenges some deeply held beliefs I have: "I cannot heal myself. I need an expert to do it." "Healing cannot be that simple, that easy." And, "Don't trust Rita that much. This is too woo-woo. She is too out there." Feeling self-conscious, I give it a try.

I lie on my massage table in the blue room. I place my hands over the right side of my lower abdomen and pelvis. *I feel into the craniosacral rhythm. The motion lightly travels between my relaxed palms. I place my attention with the sore area on the right side of my sacrum. I picture the joint between my sacrum and right ilium. I thank the joint for working so hard for me. I need safety here, stability. I wrap the joint up like a cocoon. I picture my psoas muscle under my hands. I tell her how strong she is to hold so much emotion for me and still do her job. "Thank you for keeping me safe, for protecting me, for storing these feelings I did not know how to have. We are safe now. You can let go. You can rest, relax. You can cough up any old beliefs and feelings you don't need." She starts choking up black oily gunk. I picture a string that the gunk can follow down into the Earth. I offer her golden light in exchange, however much she wants.*

Anna and I talk about transmutation. I am to build a transformational container. I think of Calvin, of Calvin and Hobbes. He builds a transmogrifier out of a large box and turns himself into a tiger. I picture a cocoon, woven out of grass, boat shaped, open at one end like a papoose, a safe nest where the seed sprouts, where the caterpillar becomes butterfly. That week, I come down with a cold. I have a shiatsu massage and the cold is gone. I have a day when everything makes me laugh. My ear is clogged. I put in drops. Then I cannot hear at all. I find this hilarious. I'm sitting on my porch and a hummingbird hovers right in front of my nose. Again I have moments where the ordinary world around me appears extraordinary, beautiful, and I am filled with gratitude. The fantasy and romance novels I read start commenting on my life, start fitting in seamlessly to what I am working on at the time. Guidance comes in every form. All the rules and separations my mind constructs are false, ideas that *this* matters and *that* doesn't, all false. I don't decide what is relevant, "They" do.

7/17/2007
My dear Rita,

I was sitting at breakfast yesterday and I looked down at the dark red-purple Marion berries on my waffle and almost cried at how beautiful they were, how wonderful they tasted, and how grateful I was to have them to enjoy. And I think you are crazy... :)

I made my cocoon. It is a little papoose boat, woven out of grass onto a curved stick. I put the sea-colored wool inside and it is so wonderful. I love to make things but I have always stopped myself because I didn't know what they were for – like what is art for anyway and why would I do it? Well, duh, art moves energy. I held it while meditating this morning, feeling a figure eight of energy moving between my hands and through the little sea-grass canoe, and knew I was part of something extraordinary – or perhaps the most ordinary thing there is, just not believed and hidden when you are not looking for it.

The first day I started my cocoon I pulled the Spider card. And outside in the yard where I started weaving it, there was a spider under the table carefully working on her egg sack. And this morning, when I sat down to meditate for the first time with my finished cocoon in my hands, I pulled the Butterfly card.

I have always thought the books I liked to read were somehow superfluous to my life – like extra meaningless fluff. But EVERYTHING is relevant and meaningful. I am reading *Sunshine,* by Robin McKinley, about a woman named Sunshine who wakes up to her magic power on her own, without training. She dreams how it works. At one point, without explicit guidance and not sure what she should do, she finds and rescues Constantine, the hero, a vampire, in this dark, formless void space, by latching onto the idea of him and following it. She calls the space "nowheresville." When she asks later why she did not receive any training in magic like other people gifted this way get, she is told, "What if you had been apprenticed, and learned there is no way though nowheresville?"

So here I am doing something I think is somehow outside of my work, or a break from my work, and I am doing explicit work right here. It is our learned beliefs that keep us here, suffering and hitting our heads against the wall.

- Keelin

Walking With Animals

I used to, almost exclusively, have negative, anxiety producing thoughts. I'd see something at random, like a truck in the road, and on autopilot, think something terrible or fearful about it, like picturing the truck hitting my car. Now I have moments of spontaneous hope and joy. I see a picture of a desert oasis on the calendar and feel a sense of hope and beauty. I expect to see hummingbirds. I find perfect shells at the beach. I begin to walk with Horse and Black Panther, to experience their company in my daily life. I have been these animals, their guidance and support familiar. I see Horse on my right side, feel his strength, gentleness, affection, vigilance, trust. I see Black Panther on my left, her fierce protection, her joy in her body. She stalks between parked cars as I walk down the street, running and leaping just for the fun of it. I write a story about her. I know I have been her, and inhabiting her body makes sense.

Sera

My claws keep hold of the edges, digging into the warm bark, the limb just wide enough for me to rest down on my belly and peer over the side. Through the dark, I can clearly see the trail the small, brown-tailed deer use to get to the river. I wait. I am the tree, part of the wind, anchored in the earth, quiet as stone, black as night. I wait. My tail twitches, the only sign of my hunger. They will come in the night, after the heat of this day, they will come to the cool water. I wait. I watch the path with glass-mirrored eyes, my ears turned to the stir of the wind.

An army of blackbirds settles high above me in the canopy, arguing loudly enough in the night air to rouse the mountain from its long sleep. The racket further hides my presence, so I don't mind, too much. A porcupine and her young pass below, heading for water. I am not as yet that hungry, so I wait. Though I feel strange this night since I woke from my nap on the sunbaked ledge, uneasy, restless, I am hungrier yet. So I ignore the new ache low in my belly, deeper than my hunger, the agitation crawling under my skin.

This night is moonless, good dark for hunting. A beetle crawls down the branch, pausing when he encounters my paw. He swivels one way and then back, trying to find a path around this massive, unexpected boulder in the trail. I lap him up with my tongue, crunching his iridescent body in my back teeth. Good, but gone too fast.

A loud crashing through the brush signals a boar on the trail, hard to miss. The thunder of his passing silences even the blackbirds for a time. I have seen what a boar's tusks can do to my kind – but I have never seen one climb a tree. I am safe on my perch, no need to move, to run. I wait. My belly growls, my tail swishes right, left, right. The night walks on overhead, the stars spinning in their God-hewn courses.

Their scent betrays them first, my nose taking in the earthy smell of leaf-eater dung and the oil in their brown-furred skin. My ears twitch back and I hear the dry leaves rustling under their tiny split hooves on the forest floor. I am a good hunter, my mother taught me well how to survive, to thrive, to live. You are of the forest, she told me, and the forest is enough. The trees are enough, the deer are enough, and you are enough.

I was too young the first time she took me hunting. I think I bothered her so much asking to go that she finally gave in. I was so excited I could barely sit still much less be quiet. But then we waited and waited in the tree. The night seemed to go on forever. I had to be very still and my legs hurt and I was hungry and I wanted to go home. I was just dozing off when the deer arrived. I was so excited all over again I lost my balance on the limb. My mother quickly grabbed me with her teeth and front claws and dragged me back onto the branch. I was smaller then, half her size at least, the ground was too far for me to fall and land safely. We did not eat that night. But this night, I will.

The rustling is close now. I can see the first brown and white speckled back below. I wait and more move by, their long ears swiveling back and forth, alert for danger, but I am silent, hidden in the leaves above. I crouch up from the limb, bent to spring, and leap onto the back of the smallest near the tail end of the herd. My teeth bury deep into the muscles of her neck as I thrust my weight to the side to bring her down. My claws dig into her hips and shoulders. We crash to the ground and the herd scatters, bounding for the river. Before my prey can right herself, I have her by the front of the neck, dragging her thrashing and kicking, off the trail and over to the base of my tree. I crouch low, my jaw clamped on her throat, and wait for her life to ease.

I thank her for giving herself so that I may live. The forest is enough, I tell her gently as she struggles, the forest is enough. When her thrashing stills, the rasping sound of her fight to breathe finally quiets, I wait a bit longer, my jaw aching from clamping down so long, my neck straining with the effort to hold her still. But sometimes you think the deer is dead and you let go and before you know it, they spring away, only to slowly bleed to death somewhere else in the forest – so I don't eat, and they don't live. I have learned to be careful, and patient.

The blood from her neck seeps onto my tongue and finally my hunger takes over. I drop her throat and tear into her shoulder with my teeth, pinning her side with my paw to pull free a long strip of warm, wet muscle. In my haste, now that the hunt is over and I am free to eat, I swallow the delicious flesh whole, the deer's warm, red blood soaking my chin and chest. While I eat I hear the two young males behind me, waiting to feed. They crouch at the edge of the undergrowth, where the tree's massive roots splay out to dig under the soil. They are not much younger than I, but they will wait, an older female's prerogative, and my kill. They slink back and fourth, growling, and soon I have had all I can eat. My belly uncomfortably full, I back away from the fallen deer with a warning growl to the males. I leap up the other side of my tree while they tear into what is left of my kill, plenty for both of them.

I climb high, as high as the tree will carry me, till I can see the stars clearly spread to infinity. My back to the trunk, I lick my fur clean, as much as I can reach of my neck and chest, lapping the dried blood from my feet, between my pads and claws. I clean my back, the fur on my hips, my belly, then between my hind legs, the odd unease I have felt there all day now a dull ache. I lick and rasp the area with my tongue, trying to get at the itch. Eventually the adrenaline from the hunt drains, I am tired, sated. I lie down on the branch, two legs dangling from each side, my chin cradled on the limb, and I sleep away the morning.

The sun at its peak, the forest music suspended in the heat, I move to the ledge, high on the side of the mountain, to rest 'til nightfall. The warmth of the rock seeps into my skin, muscles, bones. I spread out as far as my limbs will go, dozing. The shadow of Great Mountain glides in earthtime over my body.

In dreamtime I cross the river, never daring such in my waking body. I pad along through the trees, rubbing and scratching my face, then the ribs of my side, on the rough bark. I mewl and moan as I scratch, a continuous yowling I cannot help nor hold back. I lift my tail and rub my sex across the rough ridges of the tree trunks. One moment I am alone in the small clearing, the next he is there, sitting quietly, watching. Firecat! Eyes deep brown and flecked with flames, coat dark and shining obsidian. And huge, easily half-again as large as me. I shrink back into a low crouch, baring my teeth, my deep warning growl squeaking out as high-pitched whine.

"Easy there, little one." He says gently, right into my head, his voice the most beautiful sound I have ever heard. He remains sitting calmly across the clearing, but the hair on the scruff of my neck stands stiff. I try another growl, pathetically somewhere between a wail and a plea. The voice flows again in my head, warm and resonant, "Iyasa raised you well, little Sera. I can see her cunning and patience in the gleam of your coat and well-fed muscle." I start to cry, sobbing quietly, as he continues to speak. "You honor her with your every breath, female, living with courage and grace. Our forest is blessed with your spirit. You come to me now in need. Your body calls to me. Lovely Sera fear not, for it is changetime, and I will answer."

I wake as the sun falls behind the mountain. There are edges of pink and orange layered high in the thin clouds, against a sky of deep blue. Even in dusk, the stone ledge still radiates the sun's power up through my paws and belly. Firecat's answer comes just as the sliver of new moon sets over the river. I smell the male climbing down from the other side of the ridge. His scent calls a keening from my throat and I pull my belly across the rock, mewling, rasping my body over the stone, and then rolling over to rub my back.

He drops silently onto the ledge behind me, staying just out of reach should I swipe at him. He growls, a low vibration in his throat like a deep purring, and circles back and forth. I yowl again and raise to a low crouch, looking over my shoulder at him as I lift my haunches in display. The male is big, sleekly muscled, old scars cross his ribs and chest through the ebony coat, one ear nicked and bent. I slowly lift my tail aside, the end twitching. He watches, eyes the bright green of spring grass, and silently pads closer. He growls, a warning this time, and reaches out with his nose right under my tail. I cannot help it as my sex flexes, the lips flaring open, and he licks me, his tongue rasping across. I push back with my hips and spray, mewling and rubbing my face against the rock. He laps up the spray, taking his time, his tongue licking up my legs and between them, under my tail.

He crawls over my back, taking the scruff of my neck in his teeth. And so I am held while his body enters mine. He pushes quickly in and out of my sex and I yowl and mewl, my throat opening to the forest as my sex opens to this male. He finishes and pulls us both over to lie side by side, his heavy paw over my ribs, my haunches tucked into his low belly. He licks the tender skin of my neck where his teeth held me still, and I fall asleep to the soothing rub of his tongue on my back.

You Are Magic

I dream my trainer sends her mother to check on Ross. *I say no to her. Then at work I find out there are orders from six months ago that are not done. My boss takes me to her house to work on them. She expects me to pay for them myself. I say no to her.*

I dream my trainer argues for me to come back to the barn and ride again. *I have worked so hard to get where I am, why am I throwing it all away? I am wasting Ross' potential. He needs physical therapy. I say no. She has another horse for me to buy. He is white with fuzzy feet. I fantasize about being at the barn again, being a part of the community, all that I miss. Then it's Christmas. My trainer and I are in a hotel room with Amy Tryon, our local Olympian. My trainer waves me closer as they talk. I lean against her arm, my mouth against her skin. She shrinks back until we are just touching, so she can hold onto me while she talks to Amy. I feel privileged to be so close. I soak up the special attention.*

I dream my birthday party is larger than expected. I walk around and feel I know myself, who I am as a whole being. Ashton Kutcher tries to dress me up in a "gang headdress" so I can be "one of the guys." I enjoy the camaraderie but I take off the headdress.

Now, most of the time, I interpret everything that happens to me as guidance and energy processing through me as I evolve. When I cannot fall asleep at night, when I don't have an appetite, rather than pick at myself, or ask myself why, I notice that something energetically is going on and I let it go. I am less inclined to examine or analyze everything. I am able to float. Negative thoughts I am aware of I do not entertain. I practice ignoring doubt. For a week I am full of rearranging. I move all the furniture around in the living room. I move plants around in the garden. In my dreams I set boundaries, say No, over and over.

I dream of new possibilities, energy coming through me, healing miracles, and the mother of creation, Turtle, chasing me down. *I am bathed in an energy field, a vibration. It comes down into my body three times. I am told it is bad but I don't believe this. It feels good, right, magical. I have healed from cancer. I hear the words "healed by*

3000%!" I walk by a pond surrounded by a broken down chain-link fence. A turtle sits on a rock near the water. He slowly comes toward me. He chews on the buttons of my shirt. I try to get away. He slowly continues after me, trying to get at the buttons.

I bounce back and forth between a new remarkable equanimity and acceptance, a new ability to go with the flow, and anxiety and fear, clinging to old habits of self-denial and recrimination. My moods are more stable than ever, but still labile. Sometimes I can't sleep and I hate it. I spend a few days worrying about gaining weight. I agonize over whether what I eat causes migraines. I fantasize that if I were vegan and ate no sugar, I would be perfectly happy, skinny, never have headaches. I know I try to control too much about my life, my body, my habits, and that this need for control comes from fear. I believe if I can control myself, I will be safe; I will be able to control getting the things I need from others.

I practice not asking myself why when something happens that I don't like. Why I have a migraine, why my stomach is upset, why I cannot sleep. Asking why is an old habit to improve myself to deserve love. The belief is, "I have to watch myself because fundamentally there is something wrong with me." In this case I hope to deserve perfect health. I can be perfectly healthy if I try hard enough, earn enough merit. I look for something I did wrong for which I am being punished. I have no hard evidence for the reasons I find – the why is simply a practice in negative thinking. It doesn't help. I cannot count high enough, measure enough variables, to know definitively why. I choose one or two pieces of the picture and decide I know what the whole means. I act based on this tiny, partial picture, an idea created out of fear. Deciding in any final way what anything means creates limitation. I want to be fluid, move with change, and trust. My brain is not capable of seeing a web complex enough to understand how my life works, how it intertwines with others, what my life means on the deepest levels. I can feel the answers here, but I cannot measure them. It is a different kind of knowing.

I discuss discipline with a fellow massage student. She fears letting go of the things she makes herself do, like exercise and dieting and meditation. She fears she will get fat and lazy if she stopped pushing herself to improve. I want to believe I don't need rigid discipline. I choose to see every aspect of my life and situation as exactly what I need in this moment to learn and grow. If some part of it needs to change, I will feel that need and naturally take steps for the change. I don't want the need to change to come from a rejection of myself in the present, from fear, self-hate, or a desire to deserve something in the future like love or perfection.

I try to explain my sense of surrender to my fellow student. If I choose to follow guidance from God, if I accept in the moment that I am as I am supposed to be, then I need not *make myself* do self-improvement activities. I do not need improvement. I need only follow the guidance. I read *Starman*, by Sara Douglass. When Azure finds out she is a God, she is told that she is magic. She does not have to perform it or do it, just be it. All she need do is accept herself as she is and her being does the magic. Discipline then becomes listening deeply to what feels right to do. The path, my journey, is full of ease when I am in the center. I need not make myself do anything. What needs to be done will happen naturally without resistance or any artificial drive forward.

My fellow student's fears and hidden beliefs are an old pattern I wish to release: *"I will get sick if I do not diet and exercise. I will get fatter. I have to measure how large my body is, monitor my weight. If I do not watch my body, it will grow out of control. If I do not rein in my appetite, I will not stop eating. I have to make myself go to sleep at a certain time. I have to drink 8 glasses of water a day. If my body will not sleep when I decide it should, or eat what and when I decide it should, I have to make it do so for its own good. The body does not know what is best for it."* I won't find out how much my body knows unless I trust it a little − let it run the show and see what happens. Ultimately God is in charge of my shape, my health, and what I am here to learn.

Being My Own Mother

I get a migraine. It's not time for my period. It seems extra unfair to have two of these headaches a month. The pain makes it difficult to work with my mind. I feel negative, impatient, sad. I blame myself for my mood. I get caught up in feeling fat and ugly, defeated and despairing. I do not believe these thoughts but my suffering exhausts me. The strength of the negativity is surprising. I practice letting go of the why but it's hard. I try to float, but I don't want this pain.

I do an Osho Card reading:

*Problem: **Compassion** – Jesus goes into the temple and chases out the money exchangers with a whip. Buddha teaches, "For an unwounded hand may handle poison."*

*Let in: **Becoming Centered** – This is the story about the young monk who cannot be swayed by the courtesan.*

*Let go of: **The Gates of Heaven** – This is the story about the samurai insulted into a killing rage by the master. The point is heaven and hell are in the mind, created by the way we think about a situation.*

*Solution: **Death** – A woman's child dies. She goes to Buddha to ask for a miracle, to have her child back. Buddha tells her first to go into the village and collect some mustard seeds. The seeds must be from a house where no one has died. The woman goes to all the houses in the village but she cannot find a house where no one has died. She realizes everyone has lost* *someone to death. She learns that her child's death is not a personal pain but a human one.*

*Insight: **Challenge** – A farmer makes a deal with God: If God will give him perfect weather, the farmer promises to end hunger for the people. God complies and the farmer has perfect amounts of sun and rain for the wheat to grow, no hard floods or windstorms. Come harvest time though, he finds the wheat have no seeds, the husks are empty. When he complains to God, confused, God explains the wheat need to be challenged to grow properly and reproduce. The lesson is, for us to grow and create, the darkness and pain are needed as much as the light.*

I understand from the cards that my body is my teacher, my pain, my teacher. **Become centered** there, present with the pain, and I will learn. As thunder and lightning make the wheat fertile, human pain creates knowledge, strength, self-awareness, compassion, capability. The migraine is not my personal cross to bear. Everyone has pain and discomfort at times. Everyone experiences hardship and disappointment. Everyone faces **death**. My **challenge** is to see pain is a part of my journey as a human being. I am wounded so I may become unwounded. So I may cultivate **compassion**. Being unwounded is not the same as not being wounded in the first place. My journey is to be healed, to know wounded and unwounded, and to know step by step the path from one to the other.

The **gate to heaven** is this mind shift, from suffering to understanding. My work here is to open in the face of pain, to sit beside it, befriend it. To realize it is my story about the pain, not the pain itself, that causes my suffering. My mind tells me the pain is unfair. It is evidence that I am unworthy of health and happiness. My mind's story about the pain is not the same as the pain. My body is external to me, to the center and essence of Keelin, to who I am as a part of evolving God. The migraine is simply another life circumstance. In pain, I can be in heaven or hell depending on how I react to it, what I allow myself to believe about it.

Mid-August, Rita stops responding to my calls and emails. She won't tell me what happened, nor can I get an appointment. I feel abandoned both as a friend and as a client. I am disappointed but my expectations are unfair. She taught me so much and I expect her to live up to what she teaches perfectly. As I get to know her, I cannot handle realizing she is just as human and stuck in her stuff as the rest of us. When she eventually contacts me, I don't trust her. I end the relationship. I have given her too much power in my life and she took that power. I don't want to do this anymore as a client. I want to be able to be vulnerable and learn, and still retain my power. As a bodyworker myself, I want to hold my client's trust and vulnerability carefully, without taking their power. Anna models this for me. She doesn't need me to need her. She doesn't need to be my expert on anything. I want to be able to offer that for others.

My friend Ellen tells me about a craniosacral therapist, Todd, who teaches locally. I make an appointment with him to see if I want to take his workshop. The night before the appointment I dream I go for a first appointment with a famous male craniosacral therapist: *He practices in a house of young artists, though he is middle-aged. He expects our session to occur on a couch in the living room with his housemates coming in and out. He does something to my feet, then asks about my scar. What scar I ask? I have to ask twice to get his attention. He means the scar from my dream, the dream where I am slashed across the belly with a knife. Two women come to sit on the couch to discuss my scar and I tell them I am not comfortable having my emotions out in this environment. I want privacy when I receive craniosacral therapy. He decides to find a private room. While we wait for the guy with the key, he places his hand around my heart and I fall forward against a railing. The energy flooding my chest feels wonderful.*

At the appointment with Todd I feel absolutely unselfconscious. Absent is the vulnerability, sense of separation, isolation, weakness and dependence I have experienced on the table in the past year. I feel he and I are equals in healing my body. I simply have my process. I writhe, cough. My hands start vibrating. I put my hands where they need to go on my body. I feel powerful on the table and absolutely okay being me, feeling what I feel, moving how I need to move. My hands follow a spontaneous sense of how to move just like my thoughts do in sessions with Anna. There I follow where my thoughts lead, here I follow where the motion leads. I am plugged into God, into my place as me within the whole. Horse and Black Panther are there with me. I feel grateful, blessed. I decide to take Todd's workshop, to be held in October at a local retreat center.

I tell Anna about feeling abandoned by Rita. We talk about mothers and mothering. I wanted Rita to have all the answers and be perfectly capable, the mother I wish I'd had, a mother who does not exist. I realize I don't want to look for mothers anymore. I need to be my own mother, have God be my mother. There is not a human on the planet that can be that perfect. And it is too late. I am a grown woman. It is time to stop searching for someone else to mother me and do it myself.

I visit Ross and think about my own mothering. I feel painfully insecure about my ability to make good decisions for him. I find being responsible for him exhausting. In the same way I wanted perfect safety from Rita, I believe I should be able to provide perfect safety for Ross. I used to rely on my trainer to take that burden. I wanted her to mother me as well, to provide that perfect knowledge and safety for me and my horse, to always know what to do.

These relationships – my mother and me, Rita and me, my trainer and me, me and Ross – all have uneven power dynamics. I give my power away to these "mothers" and then blame them for not being all-powerful, for not providing absolute safety and all the answers. And when I mother, I take power away from Ross, trying to assume the burden of his life's journey myself.

I am learning that all creatures have their own power to express fully through their lives. I cannot take another creature's life path and direct it because then I would be stealing their power. There is not supposed to be perfect safety. There would be no creation, no fecundity, no wheat seeds, without adversity. Ross has his own pain and hardships to manage. He has his own wisdom. I can only do my best to care for him. I feel I have failed Ross because he got hurt and I was unable to fix it. But Ross and I are equal beings in the face of God. Ross has his own work to do, his own journey to make. I need not overstep my basic responsibility for him as my horse. *So relax, mother, feed him, shelter him, look out for his heath, love him well, as you know how, and let the rest go. Hold space for his freedom and then get the hell out of the way.*

Vibrating Up

I look up from meditation one cloudy August morning. A crow sits on the power line outside my window, staring at me. Walking to my appointment with Todd, I follow crow feathers; pick up one or two every block, all the way there. I am delighted, full of magic. In my blue room, the left over green-sea-colored wool from the cocoon project sits on the lower level of a table. I plant the crow feathers there. They spin in the wind from the open window, making a spiral out from a center point. I look up Crow in the Medicine Cards and find it is about walking your talk. When I trust my own sense of inner truth and allow it to guide me, I become a transformative force in the world.

Anna asks me to create a physical manifestation of the gifts I give to the world. I see my work is for me to embody the dark and the light at the same time, to live fully in the manifested external world of Mother Earth and fully in the internal world of God in each moment. I am to live the paradox of duality, of yin/yang, such that my *being* is transformative. I draw the picture in color:

One morning I choose **Butterfly** from the Medicine Cards. Butterfly is about Transformation, specifically inner transformation like changing the mind's perspective. The text suggests doing a Butterfly Spread at this time. For this type of reading I choose four cards, one for each direction and stage of a Butterfly's development. East, the Egg card, tells about the issue in gestation. South, the Larval Stage, speaks to the issue in action. West, the Cocoon, offers information about the issue's higher purpose. Finally, North, the Butterfly stage, speaks to Great Spirit's view of the issue. I don't ask a specific question but am looking for information about where I am in my life in general.

East: **Raccoon** is about right mothering; having the ability to help others without dependency or vampirism; without needing them to need you.

South: **Spider** is female creative force, the weaver. She takes the various possibilities in life and manifests. She warns that if we are not careful in our choices, especially about what we think and believe, we may create the future out of fear and limitation.

West: Weasel is the spy in the conversation, hearing the meaning behind what is said and seeing the underlying truth. She is more powerful than people realize.

North: **Black Panther** creates the courage to face the void and live, to receive healing and confront fears so you live expressing your full being without shrinking.

The reading feels like an absolute confirmation of my Blue Fire work. **Raccoon** confirms my instincts about mothering. I want to mother by sharing power. I want to honor myself and the other equally while managing appropriately the inequalities of our life circumstances or knowledge. **Spider** tells me I am on the right track in working with my mind to manage fear and make non-fear-based decisions; that creativity comes from setting aside fear and going forward into the unknown. **Weasel** tells me where I have been and where I am going. I have always been the quiet observer. I sense my powers of observation will soon allow me to see the truth within a situation as it unfolds. **Black Panther** reconfirms the heart of my work. My job is to look into the darkness, where I fear to go, to learn to accept the gifts there to illuminate the truth.

I experience a first conscious sense of my energy shifting "up," or as Anna would say, my vibration moving to a higher level. After an appointment with Anna I feel funny, disoriented. My head is too big. I feel I must have taken in too much during the session and overdosed. Afterwards, again like the first session, I go home and have to go to bed for the afternoon. I spend a few days in this disoriented state. Like my head is a big open clear bubble. Everything in life seems a little further away. A week or so later the feeling is gone, back to normal. I wonder if I have lost something, but I think the energy has simply incorporated. My cells shift up to match the new vibration. When the shift is complete, the new energy no longer feels weird or out of sync with me.

I make an appointment with a naturopath who does Mayan Abdominal Massage. These techniques are reputed to help the female reproductive system. As my migraines are mostly hormonal, I hope this will help. I have never before seen a naturopath. The massage entails deep strokes to the abdomen and pelvis, first up from the pubic bone to lift and center the uterus, and then across the rectus abdominus from the tip of the sternum to around the belly button to release old holding and tension in the belly. The massage hurts like hell. I cry and sob in spasms as she digs into my abdomen.

Seeing the naturopath does not wholly feel right, does not have the ease I associate with my right path, but I don't want to have migraines. She gives me a lot of homework, a diet to follow, castor oil soaks to the belly, lymph drainage sponging, and self-massage. I am resistant to all this self-care work. I don't believe healing has to be a lot of work. And the massage hurt – I don't think I have to be hurt to heal. But I still think that if I can just find the right thing to do, heal in the right way, I won't have to have migraines anymore.

I dream I drive our car up a snowy road. *I stop at a blocked tunnel. There is a wrecked oil truck in the way. My husband and I take cover behind cement walls while my trainer's husband blows up the truck to remove the blockage.*

I dream we have guests in our house. *They are having a party without my husband and me. My husband won't tell me why they are here. He won't give me a straight answer. Furious with him I leave him in the hammock in the back yard. On the table (a tablecloth on the ground in the yard) I walk across and knock over the apple juice with my foot. I cannot find any more apple juice in the house. My aunt is having a meeting there, in the house.*

My dream shows me I am opening up blockages in my body. My old survival habits, learned from my family and locked in my tissues, are having a party in my body without me. I fear my husband won't understand. When I share my alternative health experiences with him, I get defensive and insecure. I want his support but I feel his disapproval. He says expressing support for something I am doing that he does not believe in is lying. He sees me anxious, crying, moody, upset, panicky, and doesn't understand why I would put myself through these things. He doesn't understand why I won't just take medication. On Zoloft, I was calm and easy to live with. I haven't told him about my visit to the naturopath. I fear he will think the treatments she recommends are weird, too out there.

The next visit, the naturopath explains the connection between migraines and abdominal massage. The habitual guarding in the abdominal muscles constricts the large blood vessels underneath, reducing the amount of drainage possible from the head. Migraines are related to having too much blood in the head, causing vasodilation, inflammation, and pain. During the massage, we discuss the meaning of the headaches. I have them with menstruation, the time when my creative potential is most apparent. I bleed so I cannot hide being female. The headache relates to my feelings about being female, to my unconscious belief that I was hurt as a baby because I am female, vulnerable, because my body has holes to be filled. I have to hide this somehow, this vulnerability. The guarding in my stomach muscles, the tension there, holds this fear of being female, of revealing my vulnerability. The headache is a release valve, something has to give – I have been attempting to hide and hold myself in for so long.

I do not fully trust the naturopath, her theories and treatments. I feel grateful for her help but I don't know what to believe. I pack my belly in castor oil before bed every night and perform the self-massage. I have not gone on the diet. What they want me to eat is simply unrealistic. I want comfort and pleasure from food. I know I cannot eat only vegetables, fruits, and legumes and feel satisfied – I have tried it before. And I will not *force* myself to *do* anything. In my experience, diets never last long and feel aggressive to my body, too close to old self-hate habits, to self-denial purification habits that are actually self-destructive. I do, though, trust what comes up for me on the bodywork table. My experience of the meaning of my headaches and being in a female body feels true. I practice being kind to my uterus, ovaries, belly muscles. I make a list of positive associations with womanhood: creativity, reproduction, beauty, strength, holding, carrying, grieving, pain, endurance, transformation.

I spend the weekend with my family at the coast. My mother's sisters, brother, and their spouses come. Two of my female cousins are there, one from a few hours away, one from across the country. I have not seen either of them in years. I am the oldest. Both are experiencing significant health problems, mental and physical, causing each to have returned home to live with their parents a few years ago. I feel the women of my family hold our family's painful legacy in our bodies. In my generation, this legacy has driven me into spiritual growth and my cousins into illness. I hold a calm acceptance for my family the entire weekend. I float with the visiting, much lighter in my own reactions to them then I have been heretofore able to accomplish. Home afterwards, I am exhausted and irritable but not in crisis, not panicky like I have been after such visits in the past.

Gods on a Journey

Anna gives me a writing assignment: Ganesh, Kali, Athena and Pan go on a journey. To do this piece, I consciously throw out some old writing beliefs that do not serve me:

1) I have to write a story removed from my life. It is not okay to write about myself, I have to hide that in fiction.
2) I cannot write just how it flows out onto the page. The story has to have structure, linear narrative, fully realized background and setting.
3) I have to plan the story out, have to know what will happen at the end, before I write it.
4) I have to know who will read the story and what value it will hold for them before I write it.

I decide not to have my husband read what I write right now. He fears he will not react in a helpful manner because he doesn't understand what I am doing. He explains it like how I react to his music. He plays intricate heavy metal music. I can appreciate the art of making it, but I don't get it, nor can I offer constructive criticism. He feels the same way about my spiritual growth work.

Amina

The zoo would have been Amina's last choice for an outing with Lena and Emily, but Lena rarely came into the city, and Emily wanted to see the elephants, and the power of five-year-old desire being what it is... Amina found herself standing against the rail in the elephant house, an actual elephant behind bars in front of her, its leg chained to the wall of the concrete room, its trunk idly swiping swaths of hay into its mouth from a manger high in the corner. A sign read: "*Elephas maximus*: Common Asian Elephant."

"Each of Helga's four teeth weighs approximately 9 pounds," Lena read from the informational montage laid out below the bars separating "Helga" from the humans.

Helga? Amina thought, the very least they could have named the poor creature something Asian, like Gandhi, or Samosa. God she hated the zoo.

"What do I weigh?" Emily asked, her enthusiasm having lifted her feet to the bottom rung of the railing. She leaned over the top rail as far as she could.

"Emm, you weigh about 40 pounds," Lena explained, "but when you were born you weighed 8 pounds – almost as much as one of Helga's teeth." They laughed.

She read further, "The Asian elephant at birth weighs between 200 and 250 pounds. The baby elephant gains 2-3 pounds a day the first few months of life. And I thought you were a big baby!"

She turned to Amina, "What do you think of that? Mother of a 200-pound bouncing baby elephant. Any takers?"

"Not going there!" Amina smiled, answering as playfully as she could. Hoping her bad attitude wasn't showing too much.

"What, never?" Lena asked, surprised, "Not even a regular human baby of your own?"

"No, especially not a human one." Amina answered. She was actually grateful for her lack of responsibilities. She could do anything she wanted, anytime, and she loved it.

"You know, Amina, you're not too old. I had Emily when I was 35."

"I'm 36."

"I'm 5!" Emily added in support, climbing down from the railing and skipping on ahead.

"But women have healthy babies into their forties now." Lena argued, tailing after the girl.

"Not me." They followed Emily around the corner of Helga's cage and out the door, squinting in the late summer sun after the dim dust of the elephant house.

"You don't even need a man." Lena continued, "You can go to one of those sperm banks. Pick tall dark and handsome off a list. You know – MBA from Harvard, five Olympic skiing medals, chess champion...".

"Is that what you did?" Amina had met Lena at the Farmers Market several years ago. Her friend had gotten pregnant and had a baby in that time, but Amina never thought it her business to ask about the how of it. As far as she knew, Lena was single, ran a small sheep farm north of Deaver on her own.

"No, you've met Emily's father."

"I have?" Amina couldn't recall ever meeting a man at Lena's house.

"Yeah. I'll give you a clue. Red pickup, three-legged dog?"

Amina looked puzzled. They followed Emily around the edge of the lake and into the Aviary.

"Nubian goats..."

Amina couldn't tell a Nubian from a mountain goat.

Lena tried again, "Washboard abs...plays the flute."

It was coming to her... "No!"

"Yes." Lena was laughing now. "Oh, yes." They watched the birds, searching for the different kinds through the trees. Emily ran a little way ahead.

"Shikar? The new-agey guy at the market selling his cd's?" He usually had his shirt off and Amina would admit to his good looks but...Shikar? Could that even be his real name? It sounded like something out of Arabian nights. "He's a goat farmer?"

"Yeah, I buy his milk. How else do you think I make goat cheese as well as sheep's milk cheese? I don't have any goats."

"Does Emily know?"

"Well, yes. As much as a five year old understands that sort of thing. She calls him by name when she sees him and knows he's her dad, but she's too young to know what that means exactly."

"Do you...I mean...are you still involved?"

"Ah no," Lena signed audibly, "It was fun for a few weeks, but he's not a 'stick around the house with one woman' kind of guy."

"He didn't care that you were pregnant?" Amina was appalled – it was Callie all over again. But at least Emily knew who her father was.

"Amina – it's okay." Lena said, "It's not the end of the world. I have enough for both of us and I don't need a man around who doesn't want to be around. It was what it was – now it's over – and I have a beautiful, amazing, wonderful little girl." At that moment Emily ran up to her mother, blond curls flying, a black feather in her hand.

When they got back to Amina's one-bedroom apartment, Emily barely made it through dinner before she crashed on Amina's bed. The two women sat together on the couch, sipping last year's vintage of Three Crows Red, Lena's neighbor's label. It was the first time Lena had spent any time at her friend's place. Usually Amina came out to the farm to visit with the excuse of buying wool for Arachne, Amina's knitting and weaving shop in the city. Amina liked to hand spin and dye some of her stock, the finer yarns for knitting, the raw wool or coarser spun for weaving. People went crazy for the stuff, especially for the earthy colors she produced. Lena almost couldn't believe what people would pay for a hank of yarn, but then she knew what they would pay for her fancier cheeses, so there you go.

Setting down her glass on the coffee table, Lena noticed a picture on the end table, the cherry frame leaning against the emerald green pot of a ficus tree. She picked it up for a closer look. The woman in the picture posed in a vegetable garden, leaning against the handle of a hoe or shovel, the tool's end hidden by the broad leaves of a cabbage. She was dressed in orange-brown robes like a monk, her head shaved, one of those beaded Buddhist rosaries on her wrist. Her expression looked just like Amina's but older, her eyes wrinkled at the corners as she squinted in the sun, her tan face lined around her smile.

"Let me guess," Lena began, "Your mother?"

Amina nodded.

"She's a Buddhist monk? No way!"

"Yes, well...now she is. She's been many things."

"What's her name, or did she change it to be a monk? I heard they do that sometimes. Although come to think of it, that may not be a Buddhist thing – could be Hindu or something."

"Well, yeah, it's..." Amina hesitated.

"Oh dear, I'm offending you – Sorry!" Lena looked contrite. "Sometimes my own cynicism tends to run overboard. I'm a recovering Catholic, see. I'll shut up before I make it worse!"

"Oh, no, it's not that," Amina quickly denied, "I don't really care about religion, or at least I don't have one myself... so you're not offending me. It's just my mom... well... it's hard to explain. Her name is Callie, short for 'California,' but that's not the name she was born with. She changed it from Catherine, a nice Catholic name, you know, when she moved to California in the late sixties and became a hippie. She still goes by Callie, as far as I know, but I think you're right, the Buddhists, or at least these Buddhists, don't change their names. She lives in a Zen monastery in Monterey."

"Wow, that must have been different growing up."

"Uh, no... I mean yeah, I had a strange childhood, but not in a Zen monastery. Callie has only lived there a few years."

"You call your mother by her name? No ma or mom?"

"No. I've always called her Callie. I think she told me to. It was southern California in the seventies – we moved from commune to commune, depending on what particular religion she was into in the moment. I was raised in group living situations – you know 'it takes a village' and all that. Whatever adults were around at the time were supposed to watch me, Callie was just one of them. I don't think she believed in motherhood per se. That would have been too restrictive. Doesn't go with the whole free-spirit thing."

"Then what about your father?" Lena looked around for more pictures, didn't find any.

Amina grimaced, "Callie claims she cannot remember who he is."

A few days later, Amina had just tied off the last corner of her final piece for the Harvest Festival when her cell phone rang, making her jump. She usually kept the ringer on silent when she wove, but she was waiting for a call from her direct-trade supplier in Ecuador. Surprisingly, the phone's little digital screen said it was Callie calling. Her mother must be back from her latest month-long retreat. Amina glanced at the clock. 5:25pm, time to close. The phone beeped for a third time. There were no customers in the shop. Amina flipped open the cell and grabbed her purse.

"Hi Callie."

"Amina! You're home."

"Well, no, this is my cell phone number, remember? I am at Arachne, just about to close. What's up?" Amina's voice was less than enthusiastic. Her mother called every few months, usually to talk for an hour about herself. Amina stepped out of the shop, locked the door, and headed to catch the streetcar up the block.

"Is everything alright?" her mother asked, "You sound upset. Are you depressed?"

"No, I'm not upset, Callie. I'm fine." Amina made a supreme effort to sound warm and friendly. "How are you?"

"Oh, Amina! Everything's changed."

"Really? How so?" At the stop, she leaned against the side of a building, out of the way of the rush hour sidewalk.

"I'm leaving the monastery. I move tomorrow."

"Move where?"

"To New Mexico."

"Okaaay... what is in New Mexico?"

"My true calling." Amina kept back her snort of disbelief. As long as she could remember her mother was off every few years to the next wacky thing.

"What about the Buddha, enlightenment, and all?"

"Oh, honey, that's all in the past. I have now been called to be a healer! You see, when I was in retreat – you know we go to a place in the mountains, near Yosemite – well, I hiked up into the canyon to meditate and..."

Amina tuned out. From experience she knew this would be a lengthy story. When her mother got started, she rarely required much in response. She saw the streetcar making its way up the block and threaded her body through the sidewalk traffic to get in line. Her mom went on, something about the Owl spirit, her mother floating above her body, waves of light... Amina got on the train, lucky enough to find a seat, even if it faced backwards. She stared out the window. A few blocks down she heard Callie say "Reiki," "two thousand dollars," "it would be so good for you."

She tuned back in... What?

"What is good for me?" she asked.

"Healing. You could finally be healed." Her mother's voice said, "And that price is just while I get up and running. You'd be getting in right at the beginning. When I find my new place in Taos, it's going to be very healing. I'm going to have the grounds cleared of negative geopathic stress. They take these..."

Amina got off the streetcar at her corner and tried to catch up with the conversation. She didn't really know what Reiki was, other than her friend Alyson the LMT said it was moving some kind of energy around the body, but everyone seemed to be a Reiki master these days which made Amina suspicious.

"Wait a minute..." she interrupted something about the alignment of blue columns. "What does the Owl spirit have to do with Reiki? I thought Reiki came from Japan. Animal spirits are Native American, right?"

"Amina," Callie sighed in frustration, "this is just what I'm talking about. You make all these separations between things. I've told you over and over that this reality, these distinctions you believe in, don't exist. If you could just realize that everything is One, you wouldn't be so depressed."

Amina was so sick of this Zen bullshit.

"Great. Okay." She interrupted, "So let me get this straight. I pay you, my mother, two thousand dollars to heal me with owls and Japanese energy rays, after which I will become instantly enlightened, realize the eternal oneness of the universe, and thereby permanently cure my chronic depression and anxiety."

"You don't believe me. Fine." Callie said in a wounded tone, "I know, you think I was a bad mother. You have never been able to appreciate the ways I saved you from a life of materialistic servitude. Someday you'll be grateful."

Why were these conversations always the same? Amina climbed the stairs to her door, awkwardly digging into her purse with her free hand while keeping the phone to her ear with the other. The irony was she actually had that kind of money, not that her mother would know that. Over the summer she had been sort of discovered, thanks to some exposure at the Farmers' Market, and had sold two large tapestries from her Red and Brown series.

Callie went on, "You just don't understand what it is like for me to exist as a free being, unencumbered by the restrictions of the reality you choose to live in."

Amina couldn't resist, "Restrictions like two thousand dollars?"

There was a pregnant pause, a sniff. Ten years of therapy ago, Amina would have instantly apologized, taken it all back, made it all okay. Now, no fucking way. She shoved the key in the lock and went through the door to her apartment, closing and locking the door behind her.

"Callie, I gotta go."

She heard a nose blown, another sniff. Then her mother came back on the line, "Just think about it with an open mind. Do that for me, okay?"

"Sure. Yeah... I'm going to hang up now."

"Wait, Amina?"

"What?"

"With your permission, I'll do some Reiki on you for free. Help you release some of this negativity."

Beyond angry, Amina scoffed, "I'm not coming to New Mexico."

"No... I mean I can do a treatment for you from here."

"Yeah... whatever. Bye Callie."

Later, soaking in the tub, Amina watched the litany of negative beliefs about herself float through her mind. She assigned each of them a cloud to sit on, as her last therapist had taught her, so they would keep floating by and not get stuck in her head. In this way she had a chance at not believing them too much. The cloud-thoughts began with being 36 and single, how she'd be alone forever, moved on to not being able to remember the last occasion on which she'd had sex with an actual other person, easily passed to her too-small breasts and too-large thighs, to her loneliness. Okay, stop, that last one was a feeling. She was supposed to have them.

"I'm lonely. Amina is lonely." She said to the faucet and the candles, "I'm goddamned lonely. I'm having my goddamned feelings."

Oh boy. Nothing for this kind of mood but just to go to bed.

She finished in the tub, brushed her teeth and got under the covers in the dark. Staring at the ceiling, it occurred to her that if her mother could heal Amina long distance, then why doesn't she just heal everyone everywhere, why stop with her ungrateful daughter? The incredible thing was that when her mother accused her of being ungrateful, Amina actually felt ashamed. As if her mother made some kind of sense. As if the good mother Callie believed herself to have been was real. God, this was such a joke. Her *mother* wanted to heal her for chrissakes. That was like putting out a house fire by throwing Molotov cocktails through the door.

For a time, when Amina was around 4 years old, before the blessed structure and predictability of public school, she and Callie lived in an ashram north of Mendocino. There weren't any other kids, so Amina spent her days playing alone, wandering barefoot on the paths in the woods, playing in the creek, pretending the goats were ponies. She learned not to make noise or bother the adults, including Callie, who lived in silence – meditating in silence, working in silence. They spoke only during evening worship, when they danced and chanted together, and during weekly meetings, where it seemed to Amina they mostly yelled at each other.

Amina closed her eyes and remembered watching her mother dance. Hunger had brought her little girl body back from the creek just before dark. She'd stolen in to the main house on her way to the kitchen. All the adults were there, dancing or making the music. She crouched by the door, watching her mother. Callie wore a purple cotton dress that flared out as she spun. Her arms up, her eyes closed. She twirled so hard she pushed back the other dancers, stomping her feet and wailing. Amina didn't stay. Her mother would dance long into the night.

She ran across the dusty yard to the summer kitchen and ducked inside. The lights were off but she knew where the fridge was in the dark. More often than not, no one remembered to fetch her for dinner, so she was used to finding something for herself. She took a piece of chocolate cake and sat on the floor in the pantry, her back against a bag of rice.

"Amina, are you in here?"

It was Govinda who drove the tractor. He had a pointy tuft of brown beard like the goats. He'd let her ride on the tractor seat in front of him while he cut hay. He came into the pantry and sat beside her on the floor.

"Chocolate cake, huh?"

Amina nodded.

"Would you like to sit on my lap?"

Amina remembered most of the things that had happened to her as a child. She always knew she'd been abused, had talked about it endlessly with therapists and counselors. The talking about it didn't change anything. She knew all about PTSD, the constant vigilance, irritability, overwhelming feelings of fear and grief seemingly unrelated to anything actually happening in her life, the haunting sense that you were two entirely different people – a terrified little girl and the most capable of adults – and you had no control over which one you were at any particular time.

Ironically, it was finally remembering in detail how bad the abuse was that eventually made a difference in her mental state. The images came to her during a massage session – his penis in her mouth, down her throat, in her anus – images at once both arousing and terribly sad. It seemed while her mind had fudged over the details, her body had never forgotten what it had survived. With several more months of bodywork, the PTSD symptoms faded as her body released the memories and emotions. So now, most of the time, she was her capable adult self, with moods and emotions actually in sync with the events in her life. But she would still like to be thin.

Amina loaded the last basket of yarn into her ancient blue Volvo and shut the hatchback. The mid-September sun could be seen through the trees of the park – its broken and wavering light glanced off trunks and branches still in leaf. She felt a little like celebrating, having sold both tapestries she'd made for the Festival today and two smaller pieces, but she'd never stayed for the evening's activities before. The Festival was the last day of the Market for the season, and after closing, the farmers and craftspeople all got together for a potluck, music and dancing. Amina didn't usually feel comfortable socializing at parties, or dancing for that matter. She decided on a quick goodbye to Lena, a hug for Emily, and then she would take off.

Shikar was up on the stage when she found her way over to the party. He was playing a guitar along with the "sand candle" guy. Amina was terrible with names. She only remembered the name "Shikar" because it was so weird, especially for a white guy. Of course, "Amina" was a weird name, at least in this generally non-Muslim country. But knowing Callie, her name could have been a lot worse, like "Rainbow" or "San Diego" or something, so she didn't mind being an Amina.

She found Lena on a bench off to the side of the crowd, a corn-on-the-cob in her hand, an overflowing paper plate on her lap. Amina sat down.

"Where's Emily?" She had to wait for her friend to finish a mouthful to answer.

"She's making her own caramel apple." Lena gestured with the corncob across the semi-circle of benches to a picnic table full of kids. "If you are hungry," Lena offered, "take some off my plate. I don't need to eat this much."

Amina helped herself to a piece of cornbread, setting it on a napkin Lena dug out from under the plate. When she looked up from the food, Shikar was alone on the stage, starting a piece on his flute. The noise of the party noticeably stilled. Amina had never listened to one of his cds. She was prepared to be critical, but she quickly forgot about thinking anything as he continued to play. Yes, he was very good looking, in an "Out of Africa Robert Redford crossed with Yanni" kind of way, but she couldn't deny that the music was beautiful, seductive, lovely. A man like that would have no trouble making babies wherever he went.

Amina gave a slightly stunned look across to Lena.

"I know, I know!" Lena said, her words muffled by a mouthful of fruit salad.

Just then Emily ran up with her caramel apple poised crookedly on a popsicle stick, the apple itself the size of a softball. Amina caught it with her napkin just before gravity did its thing. She held it up while Emily took a bite, her tiny teeth skimming the caramel and nuts off the side.

The girl was into her third bite, finally to include a bit of the apple itself, when Shikar sat down on the bench across from them, having left the stage to a classic rock cover band. The first riffs from "Heart of Gold" floated over the crowd. Someone shouted "Neil is God!" and a few couples made their way to dance in front of the stage. Emily took her apple-napkin combination and turned to be lifted onto Shikar's lap, both assuming the pose with the ease of long practice.

Amina knew millions of dads held millions of little girls on their laps every day with simple, platonic fatherly love, but the sight always made Amina uneasy, made her think of sex, and paradoxically, made her envy that kind of safety and trust.

Lena set her empty plate aside and wiped her hands on a napkin. "Have you two met? Amina?" She gestured between them, "Shikar?"

"Ah, yes, Amina, I remember," he said, then added "the weaver," in a soft voice, like it was a secret just between them. Amina felt instantly irritated.

To hide her annoyance, she thought of something nice to say, "Your music is beautiful. Do you sing as well?"

"Yes, sometimes, with the guitar. But I prefer the flute."

"And Lena tells me you have a farm?"

He nodded, "Near Lake Cohoe. I have Alpine Dairys and Nubians."

"And Pirate!" Emily added.

"The three-legged dog," Lena clarified.

"He's in the truck." Shikar told Emily, "Shall we get him?"

"I'll take her," Lena offered, adding, "Is it locked?"

A shake of his head and Amina was alone with him.

After a few moments of awkward silence, he asked, "Would you care to dance?"

That was an easy one. "No, I don't like to dance."

"That's because you haven't danced with me." He smiled like he knew all about her and she didn't. He reached for her hand. Suddenly Amina urgently had to find her chapstick in her purse, with both hands. He sat back. When she looked up, she saw he had a piece of corn in his beard.

"You are a very beautiful woman."

She gave him a skeptical look, setting her purse aside.

"You don't believe me." He leaned closer again. "I could show you just how beautiful you are, Amina."

"Like you showed Lena?"

He didn't even blink. "Yes. I could do the same for you."

This time he did take her hand, then both of them. His hands were large, warm. His fingers lightly traced the insides of her wrists. She really wanted it not to feel as good as it did.

"One question," Amina said quietly, looking down at their hands. "Though it's none of my business."

"Ask me anything." He replied, keeping up the light circles on her wrist, trailing over the sensitive mound at the base of her thumb.

"If Lena, well... say if Lena died. Would you take care of Emily?"

Now he was surprised. "Of course! She's my daughter. I love her."

Amina gently tugged her hands free and looked up, at his green eyes, how his blond hair framed his tanned face, the grey at his temples, the piece of corn still nestled in the red and grey curls on his chin. "I'll think about it," she said.

She dreamed she was dreaming. She was in an old house, a mansion, with rooms upon rooms on each floor. She climbed the stairs, one hand clutched to the railing to hold herself up. At the turn of the stairs, on the landing, she realized she was naked and pregnant, her belly stretched taut, perfectly round. She had to get to the top floor, to her room, but each step was like walking through deep sand, her feet sliding back down. "I won't get there in time," she thought.

"Yes, we will, mother," her baby spoke to her, "For I can wait." She looked down at her belly, the curve of the skin an utterly beautiful thing.

"Son," she said, "Pauri," for that was his name, "How long can you wait?"

"Mother, as long as is needed." He answered, his voice holding the sweetness of a child and the conviction of a father.

She was in her room, but they had taken away all her things. No clothes, dresser, pictures, tapestries. Her books were gone, her loom, gone. Just her bed remained, in the middle of the floor. The quilt rolled in blue-green waves and she lay down in the water, floated effortlessly. She relaxed completely, let the sea hold her body, her arms and legs, her head and hair, her ripe belly, buoyed on the gentle motion of the waves. Overhead, though the outline of the rafters, she saw the night sky. Stars upon stars. Felt only relief, release, peace.

"Mother."

"Yes, Pauri, my dear son."

"Open the gate."

And she panicked, flailed about.

What gate? This wasn't it – the end? All the doing over and done?

She foundered, now sinking, for there was nothing to hold on to here. She was drowning, the water flowing into mouth and throat. She squeezed her eyes closed. Then she had to breathe, pull the sea into her lungs, knowing she would die.

"Mother, open your eyes."

The ocean flowed in and out of her lungs like air, easy as the tide washed over the rocks and flowed back. She opened her eyes. She held her son in her arms as they lay suspended under the water, still but for the motion of the sea. His large gray ears floated about his head. His trunk folded in, tucked against his mouth. In his sea-dark eyes the infinite presence of a god.

Amina woke, a slant of morning sun across her face. From her pillow she could see in the other room the corner of her loom, the prayer plant on the edge of the kitchen counter. She rolled to her back and stretched her arms above her head, arching her spine, bending her knees, letting her legs fall open on the mattress. She cupped her breasts. Felt with her fingers down over her belly, her thighs. She was open at both ends, her head, her sex, and life moved through her, the creative force of her being an entire universe quietly expanding.

She looked to her night table and saw the crow's feather Emily left behind from their day at the zoo. Amina picked it up and smoothed the barbs between her fingers. A deep, glossy black, the tapering shaft curved to the right, the base downy grey, the vane's wide edge curled in waves up to the tip. It was the most beautiful thing.

Dark Night of the Soul

I read my story to Anna. Afterwards I am shaking. I cough like on the bodywork table, like I am having a release. Anna sees me underground in the absolute dark, crawling my way through a cave, or suspended under the surface of the water in stillness, quiet. A near-death feeling. She sees Hummingbird and Cougar standing on their heads, heads underground, intentionally looking below the surface. This brings blood to the head – migraines. She mentions the "dark night of the soul." My assignment is to be a gift for Mother Earth. To allow the energy from Source, high above my head, to flow downward through my body, golden light flowing down to three feet below Earth's surface then spreading out, all around the globe. She reminds me I don't have to do anything, just relax, accept and assent. She says, "Sometimes when we see something evolving, we think we have to actively do something to aid the evolution, when really what is called for is to be an active witness for the unfolding."

The next day, before dinner, I have a sudden severe headache over my entire head and the back of my neck, pounding with my heartbeat. I cannot eat. I take two migraine pills in a row to no effect. I go to bed, ice my head, and try to sleep it off. I'm fine when I wake in the morning. I fear what Anna said about "the dark night of the soul." It seems like something bad is going to happen. I am feeling my way blind. I have nothing to hold onto, no cause and effect with which to cling.

I dream of a jury of owls. *Someone is being judged. The oldest owl is very beautiful, quite different from the youngest.*

I don't have anything to do. I'm not working and school does not take a lot of time. I have had most of the material before, to a greater depth, in nursing school. I dread free time. I resent, from when I was a small child, having to entertain myself. It feels like a burden and it hurts, having to play by myself. And I feel guilty for feeling this way. It seems ungrateful. It seems like everyone envies my free time. Yet others who tell me this consistently make choices to keep their time full and busy, and pretend they are helpless within the busyness. So everyone fears free time, fears the stopping of the doing. There is new information here. I sense I am being asked to learn how to be without doing.

I pull **Black Panther** again, about the courage to BE. I practice being. I pay attention to the moment, to what is right in front of me, release the past and the future from my thoughts. My mind does not like it. I feel uncomfortable around the doing and frenetic movement of everyone else. This prods my anxiety. My mind says I must find something to do. I must be useful, in however useless an occupation. It is more important to be occupied – the busyness hides the uselessness of what I am occupied doing.

I have a third headache within four days. My anxiety goes through the roof. I feel crazy. My abdomen, between my solar plexus and belly button, buzzes, vibrating. I'm wound up, can't be still. My blood pressure is too high. I think again about "the dark night of the soul." I fear I will be asked to do something difficult, a test more painful than I have yet faced. At the grocery store I glance at the bulletin board. A business card catches my eye. It is for a bodyworker named Sue who happens to be someone Anna suggested I see two months ago. I take it as a sign and call for an appointment.

I dream I have been kidnapped and then returned to the house of my grandfather. *I am cleaning up the blood in the sink when he gets home. The house is dark and I cannot get the blood off the sink. My grandfather has a screwdriver-like tool that works better to get the blood off. To explain my kidnapping, where I have been, my grandfather has a map showing the western states. The map includes Indian reservations. The states are all messed up. They are not in order and duplicated on the map. I assume then that I have not been raped. My grandfather makes his other daughters use the rape kit so we will have evidence. He takes one of my new, just read, paperback novels. He shows me a nick on the side of the novel. This mark means it is the same book he had with him in WWII. Someone points out that the date of publication for the book is after WWII, but my grandfather just keeps talking. He tells a story of how he'd saved this woman by giving her a third leg. I know I am special, a different child than the others – I am mostly Native American. My grandfather had been out looking for me. He'd meant to protect us, his children.*

At the appointment with Sue, I feel desperate. I still have the migraine from yesterday. My head feels too open. My body is buzzing, full of electricity. I'm scared. Barely through the door, I am in tears. She reassures me that physical changes are part of spiritual changes. My body is not betraying me.

Sue works on the left side of my pelvis. *I see Athena for the first time in human form. She stands on my right side, an old Native American woman in a full buckskin robe, her long black and gray hair has beads and feathers woven into the strands. I crawl in a cave by myself, on my knees, in the dark, finding my way with my hands. My fingers search over the cold, damp floor, the bumps, the sloped edge of the wall. Horse and Black Panther say I must crawl alone. I laugh, of course I have to do this alone, God would not make it easy. But I don't feel alone. I am simply in front. I lead a lot of people, and right behind me in the cave, Athena, Horse and Black Panther are there to support me.*

When I get off the table I feel better, less desperate, calmer, but also exhausted and overwhelmed. Tired of all this work, this weirdness. I need to be alone. I start to write a check for the session. Sue says she has a deal on six sessions if I pay $500 up front. She explains the deal is to help her clients, like me. I will come more regularly if I have already paid. This is supposed to be more therapeutic. I sense that she simply needs the money. I feel pressured and unable in my current mental state to say no. I write the check for $500 but right away I resent it. I feel like I have to come back for five more sessions, whether I need them, want them, or not.

I dream my mother and I stay in a hotel room. *At 2:30am a man comes in to check over the room. My mother is not worried – like this is routine. He wants to have a Christian program playing on the television. I tell him to turn it off. He leaves but then a lot of other people come in. The hotel manager says they need to stay in our room for a short time. My mother and I try to accommodate them politely but they are stealing our things. My credit cards and ATM card are gone. I ask them to leave. I have to yell, "Get out! Get the fuck out of our room!"*

I dream my husband and I visit a town where they are demonstrating their new elevated train. *We are invited to ride on the new line that is just finished. We ride on the train and it becomes a chairlift. The chair is hanging half off the cable. I plan to crawl off the chair carefully, trying not to drop anything, but the chair goes faster and faster until it suddenly stops at the end of the new section. A voice comes through a speaker, joking about the situation – something about good thing the chair stopped, who knows what would have happened – while we dangle over the edge. Then the chair backs up, returning down the cable.*

I dream I call to get my stolen bankcards cancelled and replaced. *The woman argues with me on the phone. She says I need to hire "Rocky Mountain Detectives" to find my cards. She says they will call me if anyone uses the cards. I argue I don't want anyone using the cards. She refuses to help me. It's Saturday, she says, too late to do anything about it. I start yelling at her, furious.*

My dreams are full of rage and confusion, fear of loss, vulnerability, people in my space who don't listen, trains not on the track, no one I can trust to help me. The morning before my appointment with Anna I wake in despair. The gate of "this is too much work" shuts tight. I tell her about seeing Sue and the naturopath, my strange physical symptoms, not being able to talk about it with my husband. She sees right to the heart of my despair: fear. She says it is okay to be afraid and adds that it is okay to be ashamed of being afraid. My fear of and shame about being afraid drains my energy and saps my will.

On the table I remember when I was three, when my mother and I moved in a large truck from Seattle to Illinois: *The first night, we stay in someone's large old house. I wake in the dark to the flash of lightning and the terrible boom of thunder. I go out into the dark strange hall, seeking the room where my mother sleeps. I find her and wake her. Annoyed, she sends me right back to my room. She says it is only a thunderstorm; there is nothing to fear.* My mother was unable to help me manage fear, or comfort me when afraid. She was often irritated when I needed help with my feelings or to be comforted. To survive, I learned to hate my fear, to be ashamed of not being able to control these feelings. If I didn't need her, I wouldn't need to bother her. I am still trying to control and contain my fear.

Fear is ungrounding. Anna suggests I actively ground and ask for support from the intercardinal directions – SW, NW, NE, SE. I can send out cables to these four corners and securely hold myself to Earth. She explains fear causes one to shrink and tighten. I can ask the energy of these direction points to help me expand into a wider space with more room. I have a contract with Mother Earth. I have volunteered to offer healing. Some of my grief, my release work, some of this is Earth healing, some of my pain, Earth pain. My willingness to heal extends beyond the borders of my body within this life. She encourages me to ask Them for self-care breaks. I am not good at this. My pattern has been to take all They will give me and then collapse in exhaustion. I want to get moving, grow fast, get on with it, but this is a process, it takes Earth time to move through, to change and evolve.

Anna says that when my husband expresses doubt and perplexity in response to my work, I can explain that this is job training. To be a healer I need to know the entire road from wounded to unwounded intimately — the joyful and fun aspects as well as the painful difficult parts. She mentions the climax scene from *The Fifth Element*, where Bruce Willis, holding the heroine, ends up holding a column of light that extinguishes the evil planet. Anna tells me "to feel a part of something much greater than perception. To allow that which is hidden in the core to be the key that unlocks all the mystery until there is no corner where the light does not shine." I suddenly realize clearly that I am the perfect instrument. I am exactly what God made to serve God's purpose in this moment. God wanted a Keelin.

Myself is all I have to be. I am just what They wanted all along.

Learning to be a Bodyworker

Mid-October, I attend Todd's four-day workshop at a retreat center in the foothills of the Cascades. The center is beautiful in the autumn rain, peaceful, nestled in the dark green Douglas fir and yellow big leaf maples on the edge of a river. The first day, giving and receiving cranial therapy, I cough a lot on the table. One of the other participants mentions that the coughing disturbs her work. I feel self-conscious, ashamed. I explain that I usually cough like this when receiving cranial work, that I am not sick. But it turns out I do have a cold by that evening, and then a migraine. I take a pill and am able to get though the second day without pain. I tell myself I am allowed to have my experience. It is okay for me and my stuff to take up some space in the world. But I am afraid the other participants won't like me. I feel embarrassed that I am sick, insecure about how I respond on the table, and ashamed that I cry so much and cough and cannot stay still. I long to simply fall asleep on the table like everyone else.

Todd teaches us to do cranial therapy through presence. He tells us not to look for movement or stillness but to put our hands on the body, feel whatever we feel, and do nothing, move if we need to follow the motion or be still. I feel validated by his method. This is how I intuitively want to do the work. He calls what we feel moving around the body *qi* (chi). He starts us each day with a qi gong session so we can practice sensing, moving and gathering qi. He encourages us to spread our awareness out, around the room, to the trees in the rain outside the window, and to seep into the body as water into the ground. There is no separation. Be the person on the table. Be the table, the room, the trees outside, the rain.

He takes us outside. *My head pounds in pain intermittently. I feel better standing still. Blindfolded, my palms are placed on the smooth bark of a small tree. I can almost span the trunk with my hands. I listen. A little rain drips cold on my face. The motion between my hands begins to spiral clockwise. I slowly move around the tree, down the trunk, following, over knobby stubs, bits of lichen and moss. I kneel, and then sit on the ground. My hands feel the base of the tree, where it roots into the earth. I want to bury my aching head in the dirt. I feel the tree working on me, awareness where my head hurts, moments of relief.*

My headache comes back with a vengeance the third day. Todd blindfolds us and we practice following him in a line. He parks each of us in front of a tree to simply listen. That evening, I am exhausted from the headache and my anxieties. I feel exposed. I cannot help but cry silently on the table, my eyes closed, when my partner works on me. I worry that Todd doesn't like me because I am so emotional, such a mess. I feel hurt that he does not come and work on me himself. He knows I have a headache. Later I confess this to my partner for the evening, who is also my roommate. She says he did work on me. I was so out of it, I didn't know. I have to laugh. I am making all this up. All my paranoia, my shame and fear, is in my head. If these perceptions have nothing to do with reality, with how other people are actually responding to me, then I have the power to change them. If I create them, I can stop.

My first evening home, after the workshop, my husband and I spontaneously make love. I feel open, not separate, my molecules spreading out into him, into the room, into Being. I am able to feel more in my body than I have before, more aroused. I feel home in my body and able to be with him sexually without irritation or frustration.

I dream a drunk man from an Eastern-European family drives his car into the top of the tree behind the house. *It is dark, night. I go outside to see what is happening. His mother offers me a lot of money to not call the police. I say no, someone has to clean up this mess. The man sits dumbly in the car, in the tree. We wait for the police. I am very angry. I yell at the guy, his mother.*

A few days later, I almost fall asleep on the table with Sue while she massages my back. I turn over and she places her hand on my sternum, her fingers pointing to my throat. I feel uncomfortable energy pushing at my throat. I ask her to move her hand. My legs are restless. I have to move them around. I am ready to be done, to get off the table. She suggests my legs are a distraction from something else going on, like my body is trying to distract me from something it does not want seen. I am irritated. I do not believe my body works in this way. I think it is a projection of how she sees the world, that it is dangerous, untrustworthy, full of trickery. I believe my legs are simply restless. Energy is moving. I don't have any hidden, dark thing I need to address.

I feel Sue pushes me through my process and I don't like it. I want to do what feels natural. I believe my body does not need to be told how to express itself to heal. I feel strongly that my body needs room to just do its thing, without manipulation or interruption. I read Hugh Milne's *The Heart of Listening*. He quotes Marion Woodman who explains the kind of bodywork that is needed is *listening*. She says the soul must be heard, respected, and given free expression, for it has been suppressed and frightened by the power needs of the therapist for too long.

This is the kind of bodyworker I want to be – to allow the body to express itself however that occurs, to trust the body to know what it needs to heal, to stay present and get out of the way. I believe any "pushing" on my part to manipulate the client comes from my needs, not theirs. I need something to happen, a breakthrough, progress, emotional fireworks, so that I will feel like an effective bodyworker. None of these things is necessarily what the client needs in that moment.

I seem to be all about No these days. At least in my head if not spoken aloud. I have sense what is right, what I want, and rather than abandon my sense of self, of what I feel is true, like I used to in the face of opposition, I am now holding that sense within new situations. When I cannot feel or do what my therapist or teacher asks, rather than think there is something wrong with me, I consider the possibility that there is something wrong with the advice or teaching. This is entirely new for me.

I go to qi gong classes with Todd. He tells us to breathe with our bellies, to not move our chests. When I try to do this I get frustrated and angry, so much so I need to cry. I simply cannot breathe deeply. It doesn't work, and forcing it runs me into a wall of anger and personal frustration. I cannot let these feelings out in class. It would be disruptive, inappropriate. After a few weeks, I decide the classes aren't right for me.

I go to a meeting where a naturopath gives a talk about animal spirit totems. With a partner we practice some cranial work and then look for a spirit animal in the other person. My partner's cranial work on me feels invasive, aggressive, uncomfortable. She tells me she sees a moose in my heart and explains the meaning of this, that moose are strong but lazy. She warns me to watch out for laziness. This makes me angry.

I don't believe in laziness. The word implies a negative judgment. I am always doing exactly what I need to do to evolve. If I am stuck, that is my process. I may need to avoid the work for a long time and none of this time is wasted. I am always learning. I must know how to be stuck so being stuck will not trigger me. I must not fear being stuck or I cannot hold space for another person while they are stuck. I will judge my clients for whatever I fear myself. To hold safe space, I must confront each fear, including the fear of "laziness," of not doing the work.

Again, I learn more about what kind of bodyworker I want to be. I think "seeing" things for other people must be done from the utmost personal clarity. Few practitioners in my experience have done their own healing work thoroughly enough to have this clarity. I, as the practitioner, must be very clear about my motives and my relationship to power. I must know why I want to look for such information for another. Do I crave power over the other person? Do I need to be the person who creates miracles for another – the person who stands between the client and "seen" or intuitive information? If I am not careful, I will project my own fears and world-view on the client with my insight and advice.

Instead, I will be like Goldman, from *Crusader*, by Sara Douglass. In his travel he comes to a rock wall with no way around or over. Exhausted by his anger and frustration, he finally sits down and asks the rock what he is supposed to learn here. Instantly he feels better, full of joy, and the rock begins to speak with him. I will not treat the body like a rock that needs to be broken or surmounted. I will not be aggressive to the body, with diagnoses and demands for information, for I sense that this can provoke the body to defend its tissues and tense up. I plan to approach the body with presence and lightness, and if it wants to talk, all the better. If not, I will still be present and joyful.

I remember my first craniosacral workshop, eight months ago. The teacher at one point worked on my jaw, her thumbs in my mouth, along my teeth, my mandible clasped in her hands. I wanted to keep my shit together in the workshop, but while she worked I felt like crying. To calm down, I pictured my baby self and held her. I told her she was safe and that I loved her. When the teacher finished the work, she asked me if elephants were important to me, if I had an affinity for them. I said no, not really. She explained that while she was working with me, she saw elephants, especially the way they care for their young. It turns out we were both thinking of the same thing – safe and cared-for young. For the teacher, elephants are associated with that idea, but not for me. If she had told me that elephants should have meaning for me, she would have been wrong. Elephants were her interpretation of what happened between us. I feel strongly that my future client have her own process. I will support that process, offer insights and possibilities, but ultimately the truth of her experience is hers alone.

Calling for a Truce

I wake one morning craving chicken. I have been a vegetarian for twenty years. Suddenly it's over. I want to tune into and follow how I feel rather than follow old rules I have set for myself. I became a vegetarian at seventeen when I saw a deer that had been hit by a car run off into the woods with its leg hanging off. My refusal to eat meat was my refusal to accept that this happens in the world. I feel differently now. Seeing such an event again would hurt, but I can accept the pain now. I see that pain is a part of what we are all doing here on Earth, animals included. Suddenly I see my refusal to eat meat as the same as my refusal to play the game of being human on Earth. Pain is a part of the game. Taking my place as an omnivore, as responsibly as I am able, feels right. I am ready to play my role. I pull the **Antelope** card. Antelope says to the people that they should eat him and nourish themselves, for that is his service, his way to evolve. Being willing to live interdependently, such that animals die so I may live, is part of *my* evolution.

I vacillate between new experiences of health and illness. Some days I have an amazing sense of well-being and abundant energy, feeling better than I can ever remember experiencing before. Other days I have several new and old physical symptoms and I feel my body is attacking me. I have back pain on the right side of my sacrum, and between my right scapula and my spine into my right shoulder. I am easily exhausted. My stomach is upset and gassy. I am not digesting my food. I have heartburn at odd times of the day, whether my stomach is empty or full. At night when I lie down to sleep I burp repeatedly. I wake in the night with my heart racing, my belly hyperactive, bubbly. I heat up in my sleep, kicking off the covers in our 50-degree bedroom. I get migraines twice a week with intense emotions of frustration, anger, fear, and hopelessness. On the advice of the naturopath, I start taking homeopathic remedies. It seems all I do is go to appointments – Anna, Sue, Todd, the naturopath for Mayan Massage, an LMT for shiatsu, and don't forget the chiropractor.

In response to my digestive problems, Anna and I talk about cows, how they have four stomachs. They hold the grass inside themselves long enough to digest the tough fibers. I feel my abdominal organs, my diaphragm and stomach, vibrating and buzzing during this discussion. I sense "They" are working on my belly as we speak. I am holding things inside long enough to process them, to get what I need from them.

I dream I look for my room in a big resort complex built on a slope. *My mom is hosting a group event there. I have my key. I look at the number, 269. I cannot find this room. I look at the key again. It may be 261 or 102, I can't tell. I go around to the other side of the complex. I think this part looks more familiar. I find the walkway and bridge to my room. I look at the key. The number changes before my eyes and then disappears. I see my face, my dead face, in the key. I am not frightened. I am curious about this sign, what it means.*

Todd works in the area of my liver. I have a headache and jaw pain. My right upper back and shoulder are sore and locked up. During the session I feel increasingly angry and irritated. I picture my father in my head and rip him apart with my hands. I don't want to be a person who was sexually abused. I want to be normal. I want to work with men without being triggered in this way. My feelings about Todd during this session are confusing and disturbing. I want his attention. I fear behaving in a way that would cause him to reject me or ignore me. On the table, I wish he would touch me in a pleasurable, sexual way, but I don't want to have sex with him. I want his safe, magical hands and his attention to heal my sexual self.

Anna suggests I put my sexual abuse story in a container. In this way I can control the flow of information from this part of myself so it does not interfere so much with my daily life. I can open the container at regular intervals in meditation, see what arises, and then close it back up. I can have another container for my feelings. All my grief, anger, frustration, fear, all go in the container. Feelings are good compost for the seed from which will grow my future work in the world. When I get home, I place my baby teeth in a jar with a lava rock from the beach and a picture of a sexy man torn out of a romance novel – my child, the earth and fire, and sex into a jar. I place a lovely round handmade pottery bowl with a lid on my altar for my feelings, composting them to feed the future. I pull **Frog**: tears purify the soul.

I dream I go to an appointment with Anna/Sue. *She has invited a guy to my appointment. She explains he will help. She tells me that while she was on vacation in New York she meditated for me and it was about sex and she became aroused. The guy starts talking first. He cries about his girlfriend in another state that he left to come here. I am angry. Why is this guy taking up my appointment for his therapy session? I realize I have already done the work Anna/Sue wants me to do today. I leave the room and come back. Anna/Sue has me sit on her other side when I return. She says it's time to breathe. I say I don't want to breathe. She calls me a petulant child. I try to breathe and after a struggle, am able to breathe deeply, into my belly. She says, "Good, this is a breakthrough." I am out of the room again. I try to go back in, my appointment is not over, and then Anna/Sue is in the hall with me. She hands me three pieces of paper. I see the papers contain an eastern religious explanation about the nature of love. I am angry again. I don't want religion or explanations. She turns into Anna and says, "See what is happening to you?" She wears a macramé dress. She asks herself aloud why she is wearing the dress. She holds her arms up and her thighs are exposed. She is ugly, I think, more like me.*

I receive a long-form (over two hour) shiatsu massage. Afterwards I ache all over. That night, I cannot sleep. I stay home the next day with a fever. I have back pain, kidney pain, and gut pain unless I lie down. I cannot eat. On the table with Sue that afternoon, I feel like an angry two-year old, hiding out of my body. I don't want to be here. I am in pain. I cannot remember not being in pain. I don't want to do this anymore. I want nothing to do with existence. I am mad at God for sending me here. I don't want a body. Bodies hurt, are humiliating, vulnerable, frightening, confusing. I don't feel safe in my body. I am biding my time till I can return to God, just going through the motions but not present. That evening I start my period, a week early, and get a migraine. I pass clots the size of large goldfish.

At home, I lie down on my massage table. *I invite my guides, whoever of my highest self who will come, to work on me. I invite my soul to speak to my body. Soul is angry, resentful. She says she hates being trapped here, in the body. She hates the body. She wants to go home. I invite my body to speak to my soul. Body is sad, very hurt by what soul says, and confused. She cannot go "home." She is trapped here, in existence. When the soul leaves, she will cease to exist. There is no other home than here on Earth. Body wants to be loved. There is a lot of grief here. How do I get these two to live together and not willfully hurt each other? Soul and body must evolve together, that is how it works here. The way things are, the point.*

For a week I am nauseated, hungry but cannot eat much. I wake at night too hot, my stomach burning. Anna says this is a *physical* spiritual process. I am being asked to break all sense I have of reality, let go of beliefs of what is real or not real, all the way into *each cell*. I see a body-centered therapist whom I met at Todd's workshop. On her table, I ask my diaphragm to speak. *She is angry, coughing. I scream into a towel held between my teeth. I ask my body to speak to my little girl. My body is pissed at her for leaving, for holding up the process. My little girl doesn't trust the body. Neither the body, nor the little girl, trust my adult mind, who runs them both headlong, kicking and screaming and trying to catch up, into spiritual growth and change. I jump into the void and get angry at my little girl for being frightened and my body for being slow.*

I dream I share a house with Nadia and a guy. [Nadia and I were platonic housemates 15 years ago.] I rearrange the kitchen and living room. Nadia grinds her pelvis against mine. She means to give me an orgasm. In the middle of the grinding, she says she is getting aroused. She asks if she can come instead, as she never gets aroused this easily. I say fine. She grinds on me some more. I hope our housemate doesn't hear. She comes and simultaneously throws up in my face.

Anna explains that we are in an upshift. It feels like spirit is trying to escape and the body cannot leave the ground. Somehow these two must be brought together to shift up together. She suggests I bring my foundation on Earth up to my spirit. She offers the image of a tower. The plot of Earth I stand on rests on the top of the tower. I can sit here in meditation, my feet planted in the soil, and send out four cables to the intercardinal directions to secure myself to the Earth. This way I am on the Earth and up where spirit is being lifted. This is still Earthwork. The body is slow. Cells themselves must let go of the old way. This is a process. It takes time. Form gives meaning to the expansion. Anna reminds me growth is not an illness. It does not need to be fixed or corrected. There is nothing to do about it – just be a witness. Growth is painful. Be present for the pain. My body self and spirit self are going to need to find some compassion for each other.

In *The Subtle Knife*, by Philip Pullman, Ruta Skadi, a witch, meets a group of angels. She is over four hundred years old, wise by human standards, but she cannot fathom how childlike she appears to the ancient angels. Rather than envy their wisdom or transcendent way of being, though, Ruta smells her "cloud pine" broom and revels in its rich piney scent. She rejoices in her form, that she can feel her body flying through the air and smell the tangy pitch in her broom. She even delights in knowing she will die, and her body will nourish the earth and other lives as the earth has nourished her. The angels, beyond an embodied existence, have lost something. Ruta responds to them by feeling a renewed joy and love of her material existence and intimate relationship with Earth.

I envy her love of matter. I cannot feel this way right now, but I have had my moments when I was fully home in my body. I remember last spring, when I had a few weeks where everything around me was unbelievably beautiful, when I felt a deep and spontaneous gratitude for Earth and my life with her. I am supposed to be here in existence. My job is to be embodied, to feel, to experience this. I must coax my spirit back into my body. There are rewards for being here, not just pain, but I cannot experience the good stuff when fragmented. I can only feel the glorious communion with Earth in a body. When at home in my body my life has meaning. And I sense that I can only serve Earth, act to heal Earth, in this home state. As long as I am out of my body, I am part of the problem.

Into the Underworld

My husband's parents come for a visit. We have a misunderstanding about where they will stay. We think they are going to a hotel. They think they are staying with us. This would not have been a problem except the last time we visited them, a year ago, was uncomfortable and difficult. I was anxious and emotional, sick with a migraine, caught up in my own process and fears and unable to explain, and they responded with insecurity. I needed to be alone for most of the trip and they took this personally.

For this visit I still feel defensive about my boundaries. The misunderstanding makes me angry though it isn't anyone's fault. After they leave, my husband and I talk about it. He thinks the awkwardness and trouble with his family is my fault. I tell him as long as he believes his parents are healthier or less dysfunctional than me, then he will blame me for any friction in my relationship with them. I explain that relationships take two. He cannot hold me responsible for their assumptions about me. Yes, I need to ask for what I need, but also they need to ask for information and take responsibility for their fears and assumptions.

I dream my husband and I are going out for a free dinner at a fancy restaurant on a hill overlooking a coastal town. *We dress up. There is a long wait for a table. I go to use the bathroom. I get my period two weeks early. I realize I have blood on my long yellow skirt. It takes me a while to clean up. I want to forgo dinner and go home. When I leave the restroom, I cannot find my husband. He has left me there. I go to call him on my cell phone. There is a message from him. He says he will be back at 7pm. It is 2pm. I am outraged and dumbfounded that he would leave me there because I spent so long in the bathroom.*

I confront him when he returns. He says he doesn't think our relationship should be like that – that we take care of each other all the time. He wants to be independent. I am furious. I yell at him. I go to hit him but this 1950s cop shows up to mediate. I decide to just take the car but my husband has brought a different car. I don't have a key. I throw a tire at the car. It bounces off and hits a house. I say to the cop, "I am making this worse, aren't I?" I wake still trying to argue the point about my husband not abandoning me just because I spend too long in the bathroom. I feel like I am having a release – I sob and cough. My husband holds me and we snuggle until it is time to get up.

If I take care of myself, and this inconveniences someone I love, I fear they will abandon me. If I ask for and take what I need, I fear others, especially family, will reject me. My husband's parents perceive my need for space as a judgment about spending time with them. I cannot control what they think or perceive. Amazingly my husband does just the opposite of what I fear. The more I express what I need, practice my new boundaries, articulate where I am at, no matter how "woo woo" or difficult to understand, the more firmly he supports me. We have difficulty when we don't talk about it. The minute I get over my fears and just tell him what is going on, he is right there to listen and work it out, even if he doesn't understand and has to take some time to think about it.

At my second appointment with the body-centered therapist, we talk about childhood emotions stored in the belly, primal fear and anger. On the table I feel like a stubborn six-year-old boy who doesn't want to play. I want to be left alone. I feel fiercely angry and afraid, and resigned. I don't know what to do about this, about not wanting to be in my female body, about my body not being a safe place to live. I fear I cannot do anything about it.

Expressing these emotions seems pointless. I learned my first year of life that crying didn't help. I cried and cried and did not get what I needed. So I stopped crying as a baby and now, as an adult, I cannot stop crying.

I'm tired of dealing with my childhood pain and feelings. I want to be an adult, free and capable. I'm sick of being this messed up freak that cannot leave this stuff behind. I feel my whole life has been crippled by how it started. I am very vulnerable with this therapist. I want to see where this leads but I am cautious. I don't trust her completely. She happens to have the same name as my mother. Perhaps that is too much and I am pushing my process too quickly.

I read *The Way of the Shaman*, by Michael Harner. He describes the shamanic way of being as living in two consciousnesses at once, ordinary reality and the shaman's dreamworld. The reality sensed in one or the other consciousness only makes sense within that consciousness, not in both. The shaman learns to live within the two without conflict or doubt. In *The Subtle Knife,* Pullman quotes Keats' theory of "Negative Capability:" the capacity to accept, without reaching for reason and explanations, uncertainty and the unresolved. I am learning that to heal, I need some negative capability. I practice trusting hidden intelligence. I allow the consciousness that explores my internal landscape and knows what I need to heal to do its job. I trust my cellular consciousness, my body, to know what, how, and when to release to heal. And I *consciously decide* to ignore doubt.

I don't know how to get my little girl to return willingly to live in my body. She doesn't want to be in pain, and her experience in my body began in pain, is still in pain. How do I make peace with this pain so I can put myself back together? So I can be whole? There has to be some acceptance here, a willingness to enter mystery and uncertainty and surrender. This does not mean I stop doing what is in front of me to do to heal, that I stop trying to resolve the pain. But at the same time, I need to make some space for the pain to exist, to teach me.

How do I do this? How do I be in pain, be emotional and teary, and function? Not reject the pain and emotions but live with them, make friends with them? I take a clue from Pullman's *The Amber Spyglass*. Will has to open a portal into another reality with a special knife. If he breaks the knife, he cannot open the portal and he'll be trapped. He has already broken the knife once by not being properly relaxed and focused while he used it. He was able to get the knife repaired, but that is not possible now. He is worried about his mother who is in pain and needs to be rescued. He knows if he tries to force her from his thoughts, he will break the knife. So he tries something new, he allows her room in his thoughts but makes the whole space larger, so his worry for his mother can be there *along side* his focus on using the knife. It works. Perhaps I can do this with my pain. Rather than ignore it, hate it, try to get it out of my mind, I can say, "Yes, I know you are there," and simply look another direction when I cannot do anything about it at that moment.

Perhaps I can make more room for me. I can be large enough to encompass the pain and encompass other things I need in my life as well. Then I can enter a new reality, where pain is simply a *part* of my life, not its focus. The pain can take its place among my other feelings, having no more charge to it than joy, fear, pleasure, anger, boredom. I can hold awareness of many states in my being at the same time, without contradiction. To cut a portal into a new reality the secret is to stop trying to cuts parts of myself out. I expand my awareness to encompass all parts and adjust my attention according to what I need to do. If I can make room for all parts of myself, I need not fear them, fear their exposure or feel ashamed of them. This is healing.

I am experiencing the classic hero's journey to the land of the dead, my own personal initiation, mythologized from Gilgamesh, to Odysseus, to Will Parry. The journey involves working with shame. When Will is in the boat, crossing the river to the land of the dead, he feels as if something hidden and private from his heart is being dragged into the light and it hurts. The parts of myself I hate, the parts that get in the way of my life, my fear, my childhood resentment and grief, my confusion about sex and men, I try to hide these parts from the world. I'm ashamed of them. I identify with the person who does not feel these things.

While pretending I am emotionless and needless feels safe, this identity is not real. She needs to die for me to be healed and whole. I need to look at and accept the real person I am, including all the parts I fear would cause me to be unloved and rejected if anyone knew about them. The death I face is the death of old identities. To accept who I really am, all my parts painful or not, I need to be willing to let go of who I think I am. I am not a simple being. I do not feel one thing at a time. I have parts of myself I do not want, understand, or control. I can learn to look at these parts, befriend them, drag them out into the open. My old self can die and I can move into, more fully inhabit, the complete powerful being underneath – the Keelin that God wanted all along.

Closing the Wound

The first week of December, during my third appointment with the body therapist, she has me sit on the floor between her legs. She holds me while I hold a large stuffed bunny. I was already crying while on the bodywork table. The minute I leave the table, to join her on the floor, I feel unsafe and dissociate from my body. I try the exercise because I believe she is the expert. I trust her to know what will help me. But right away I am too triggered by the position to speak up or interrupt what we are doing. My lower back is pressed right against her crotch. Though we are both clothed, this is all I can think about. She is touching me with her crotch. All my muscles freeze and I endure this like a deer caught in the headlights till the session is over and I can escape. For the next few days I am a mess, sad and teary, with a migraine. I buy a stuffed bunny for myself. This feels comforting but also embarrassing, humiliating. The next day I give it away to a friend's child. I am not a child. It is too late for me to be two years old. I need to figure out how to heal my wounded child *and* stay in my adult self.

Anna and I talk about power. How does one seek help to heal and not give away all their power in the process? As I have negotiated these frightening physical changes the last few months, I have reverted once again to giving my power away. In the body therapist's lap I felt absolutely helpless and terrified. I went right back to being a sexually molested toddler. This may have been her goal, to have me revert to the child and then try to comfort me. But instead of being comforted, I feel re-victimized.

I realize this is not the appropriate therapy for me at this time. I don't need to become a terrified baby. I especially do not need anyone to touch me when I feel this way. It is too late for me to be physically re-mothered. I don't need this wound opened and re-experienced. I need it to close and heal. Perhaps it is actually my giving away power that causes me to keep the wound open, to keep re-victimizing myself with various healing practitioners. I have always believed if I didn't do whatever therapy they recommended, that it wouldn't work. I thought I had to surrender to their expertise to benefit from it. This is my problem, surrendering to human beings. No human on the planet can know what is right for me more clearly than myself. I need to move into this truth and live it. Stop asking others to rescue me. Seek help and advice, use what works for me, but surrender only to God.

Anna gives me instructions to heal my woundedness:

1) Create a safe container for wound exploration and healing – like a harness and headlamp you might wear for spelunking.
2) Picture the wound.
3) Travel with care all the way to the bottom.
4) At the bottom of the wound there is a spark, a tiny light of your true self. Invite this light to move up and expand through the wound to assist healing.
5) As you climb up, you will run across essential parts of self embedded in pivotal moments of woundedness.
6) Gather up any parts that you need to be whole and thank any parts that decide to remain in the healed wound.
7) Behind you, pack the wound with warm moist gauze, so the tissue can heal from the bottom up.

8) Revisit as needed to unpack the wound, throw away the soiled gauze, spread light up from the bottom, and re-pack the wound as it heals its way up.

Anna stresses it is imperative to now allow my light self to rise out of the pain. Like freeing a hot-air balloon tied to the ground I must loosen the tethers and allow my light self to float up. In our culture, there is no pre-set process understood for healing the self. There is no single way that will work for everyone. If I choose to free myself from cultural constructs that define illness as mental or physical, and healing as what is proscribed by doctors and experts, then I have to be self-motivated, self-defined, and self-validated. I have to be able to support and comfort myself outside of cultural supports and comforts. I do this through recapitulation of self. Go back to those moments where essential parts of self reside and collect them so I can be whole.

I sit in meditation. *I draw a filled green circle around where I sit. I ring the circle with fire. I picture my wound, a cone shape in my torso – the point in my pelvis, the wide-open end just below my throat. The sides are pink and lumpy. I go down to the bottom. I find two wounds there: 1) I am torn from God, abandoned here alone without memory of why or who I am, without help that I can see, and I am in pain for years; 2) I needed to be held as a child in unconditional safety and love. As a child, when I was touched, it was for sex. I gather the essential parts of myself here in these two wounded areas – my strength to survive, my fierce knowledge of what love is, what it should feel like, what it is for. I thank the parts of me who wish to stay, to remember, and to mark the wounds with scar tissue. My wounds are a part of me too. I see the spark of light at the bottom of the wound. I invite the light upward, to fill the cavity and seep out into my cells. I pack the wound from the bottom up with light-filled moist gauze. I tape over the top to seal in the packing.*

I realize attention itself, presence, was missing when I was a child. My gift is to have experienced the pain of being raised by parents who were not home in their bodies and who were preoccupied with getting what they needed from the outside world. My gift is to know the difference between presence and absence; to have increased sensitivity to absence, impaired tolerance for it, and to know what presence feels like as a tangible, palpable, force in the world.

I dream Todd pulls strings of craniosacral movement from my hands. *I feel both sides of my body adjust. It is frightening, uncomfortable. When we are done he praises me. It feels very good to hear the praise.* I tend my wound in meditation every few days, unpacking, taking up my power from the past, inviting the light to move up and out, and repacking. I watch the wound slowly fill in with healed tissue.

I read C.L. Wilson's *Lady of Light and Shadows*. The characters can protect themselves with a Spirit Weave, an invisible barrier that works by convincing a trespasser that she cannot pass through it. The barrier convinces her that she is exhausted and that it would be impossible to proceed. Living wounded is like being trapped in a Spirit Weave of my own making. I built it to keep me safe, but it blocks out all the light. It keeps me safe by keeping me immobilized and convinced of my own powerlessness. The dark shadows cast by the weave talk to me constantly, telling me stories about how bad things are, saying, "Your pain is intolerable. You've been in this pain forever. You will never get out of it. You are broken." These shadow stories are totally unhelpful. They must be interrupted for any light to seep in. I have a choice about whether I listen to the shadows and follow them or not. If I follow them, I will stay in shadow. I need to find some light to follow, light thoughts. I open my Gates of Consciousness. I repeat to myself, as much as I needed to keep the shadow thoughts at bay: "I am enough." I stay aware of the shadows. I know where they are, but I know they are not me.

My body quiets down. I stop getting headaches every few days. My digestion slowly begins to work again. My upper back stops hurting. In the calm after the storm, I see that I live in my body, even when I feel well, as if my body were unsafe. This creates an internal, cellular-level energetic autoimmunity. I feel attacked from within by pain and discomfort. I live in fear of another headache, of getting sick. So my cells are constantly vigilant, constantly looking for a danger that does not exist. Anna tells me to reduce the level of panic within my body. I have these roaming particles of light in my system so activated to find danger they attack my own cells. She suggests I gather the troops and give them some direction.

I tell Anna about my dissonance with the body therapist's methods, with Todd's qi gong and Sue's pushing. I don't do my healing the way they do theirs. Anna suggests I look at my life as a tapestry I weave as I go. I will gather some strands from other people and weave them in to my cloth, take what works from what they do. But ultimately, my weave will be my own, unique, unlike anyone else's. I will not heal or be a healer exactly like anyone else. What I am called to do myself, what my heart hears as true, will be my work. It is not supposed to mimic anyone else's calling.

I sit in meditation. *I make a circle and gather my light particle army to me. Right away they vibrate so strongly together that reprogramming occurs naturally. The light wants to help but hasn't known what to do. The high level of panic in my body prompted the light to act – so it attacked itself/me. The light feels strongly of love and comfort. A wall of light appears outside my body to vaporize external threats. A beam of light roams my body to assist repairs and healing. I thank the light for its help and support. I feel intense gratitude to They and to Anna for this assistance.*

I start 2008 with my husband on a cross-country ski trip. The woods and snow in the winter sun are lovely, quiet. I feel alive, calm and content. I do an Osho card reading for the New Year:

> Problem: **Enlightenment** – The story tells of the bodhisattva vow of Buddha. A bodhisattva refuses to leave his body when he reaches enlightenment so that he may help others on their path. We are all connected so we all must reach enlightenment together.

> Let in: **Understanding** – This is the story about the two monks crossing the river, one carrying the woman, one upset about the other carrying the woman. Your own shadow is what you judge and see in others.

> Let go of: **Imitation** – A young monk copies his Master by always holding up his finger just like the Master does when making a point. The Master cuts off the boy's finger and the boy finally understands he can only be whole as his unique self.

> Solution: **Innocence** – Be mad in love like St. Francis and you will live in understanding with all beings.

> Osho's Insight: **Self-Acceptance** – This is the story of hearts-ease knowing when planted that the gardener wanted hearts-ease. God planted a Keelin seed because he wanted a Keelin.

I am always amazed at how these readings speak to me in the moment. How do I become a healer? How do I become someone who devotes their life wisdom, their own **enlightenment**, to helping others achieve self-liberation?

Own my own stuff. **Understand** that those things I judge in others are my own fears. Do my work here, on my own fears, so I don't go putting my stuff on other people, so my work with others comes from the **innocence** of unconditional love and not from my own ego needs and desires. Don't **imitate**. I am not supposed to be Anna or Todd or Sue or Rita; they are already here, doing their part. Deeply **accept** and believe that I am supposed to be a Keelin, that I am exactly what is needed.

I have a session with Todd. It feels great to simply get on the table and not have to talk or put my experience or story into words. I cry and cough. I am short of breath and then it releases and I can breathe more fully. My hands are drawn to my sternum and I work on myself. I feel peacefully unselfconscious. I express my emotions, cough and writhe; move how I need to on the table. I experience a wonderful feeling of wholeness, peace, completeness, connection and acceptance.

I dream I arrive at college for my senior year. *I walk down to campus pulling a hand truck with my bag. I want to check my mailbox. In one hand I work a piece of clay. A beautiful blond boy comes up to me and introduces himself as Murphy something. He says he is from Lhasa, Tibet. He follows me as I look for the mailroom. I remember where it is but the campus has changed. There is a mall with fast food restaurants where Commons used to be. Now they*

157

charge you for a mailbox. The way Murphy follows me I think there were no women in the monastery in Lhasa. The mailroom has a long line for the window. The window is closed with no indication of when it will open. Murphy hears someone's cell phone ringing and wanders off to follow them. I figure that is the end of our talk together but he comes back. He says there is a cost for everything here. I tell him the crowd is strange; I have yet to recognize anyone I know.

Anna and I talk about balance. About how dark and light, awake and asleep, pain and pleasure, life and death are mutually defining. You cannot have one without the other. Human existence is always moving through these dualities. So how do I make peace with this? How do I find a way to accept constant change? How do I teach myself to feel balanced when life is often off-kilter? I sense if these dualities are mutually dependent, then they are not as far apart as I think. If one is always flowing into the other, all I need do is wait, all I need do is to not resist the flow, all I need do is stay awake and learn from each state. When I feel the pain of scarcity, when I believe I am not enough, I tend to close down to keep what little I have. So switch the direction. If I can close, I can open. Allow the expansion and I will feel the abundance. Anna asks me to create something about balance. Mysteriously, I build an insect. Her name is Agapanthus:

Being the Buddha in Hell

One evening in February I get a call that my horse's lame leg is worse. The woman who takes care of him wonders if it is time to put him down. I put off any decisions until the vet can see him the next day. I cannot sleep. I lay awake, upset and crying. Eventually I wake my husband. I just start telling him how I feel, no matter how useless or irrational it seems. I sob and say, "Ross is only fifteen years old. It's not fair that I don't get to ride this wonderful horse for years. I only got to ride him for 6 months before he broke. It's not fair. I am angry. I have to decide to kill him when his leg gets too bad. How do I know when that is? This sucks. I have to kill this beautiful animal." I have never let myself complain aloud like this before. I thought it was pointless and I could not ask for another person to listen. But I feel better. I feel some movement in the pain, some relief. When the vet comes, it turns out Ross' hoof is bruised. He probably stepped hard on some frozen mud. His original lameness is not worse. He's fine.

I am learning **Snake** Medicine. My job is transmutation. Snake medicine shamans repeatedly have snakes bite them so that the body can learn to transform the poison. I find I am thirty-eight years old and I am finally learning how to grieve. Grieving is an experience I have to go *through*. Loss is a process, not a poison as I have always believed. I have to have the emotions I actually feel and express them. I see that feelings are irrational, but that does not make them useless. The point of feeling is to feel. This is the alchemy of Snake. The process is the gold.

Anna contrasts two types of parenting. A child's dog dies. The parent can hold the child while she grieves, tell her feelings are natural, beautiful. The child cries as she needs to and the grief moves out of the child, expressed into the world. Soon the child moves on, and the grief and loss is naturally complete. Or the parent can tell the child that death is a part of life, accept it, crying won't bring your dog back. In this case the child is told her feelings are useless, a waste of time. But she still has feelings. She simply doesn't learn what to do with them. So she tries to suppress her feelings and feels shame when she cannot. The grief gets stuck and stays inside her body. Into adulthood, she never learned how to grieve so every new loss gets stuffed into the same place, with less and less success. Eventually there is so much pain crammed into that place in her body that it begins to spill over into her life when there is nothing apparent to grieve about. She feels sad for no reason. She feels depressed, anxious. She has chronic illness, chronic pain.

Anna asks me why I am here. What is the purpose of my existence? My answer changes as I give it. God is no longer this place I came from that I am trying to get back to. I sense now that I am an evolving being of energy. God is not separate from me here, now. I am God evolving. All of this is God evolving. My being of core light is in a constant simultaneous expansion and concentration.

For the New Year I also do a Butterfly reading:

East: **Black Panther** allows us to face our fears and look into the dark side to receive healing and just be.

South: **Dragonfly** sees through the illusion of form, the colors of his wings reminding us of magic.

West: **Elk** survives by doing what he knows how to do. He does not run fast and leap ahead like the Mountain Lion to escape the predator, he steadily climbs, in accordance with his own nature, until the Mountain Lion tires and gives up.

North: **Buffalo** is about prayer and gratitude, about realizing abundance and living within the relatedness of all things.

I have now come full circle. I started with **Black Panther**, with a leap into the void, the unknown, the dark inside me I feared. I learn every day that there are aspects of life here that are mysterious and hidden, like the colors in **Dragonfly's** wings, but true and real. All I need do is be myself, express my true being like **Elk**, and I will survive gracefully. With **Buffalo**, I arrive conscious of all I have received, the healing and assistance, and of my interconnection to all creation.

Despite my growing ease with my life and confidence, I still have migraines 2-3x a month. I argue with myself about taking a pill or not. I suffer through with the pain trying "natural" remedies but I do not find any that help. The prescription pill often takes away the pain but leaves the nausea and fatigue. If I take them too often, though, they do nothing. The NLP therapist believes negative thinking causes my headaches. They are clearly associated with negative thinking, but it's a chicken and egg thing. Being in pain naturally causes me to hate life, but I ride the negativity much more lightly than I used to, so I would think the migraines would improve.

The naturopath believes I have food allergies such that my migraines are caused by excess inflammation in my body. I have great resistance to this answer. I have never been able to follow a diet for more than a month or two. I have wanted to be thinner since I was twelve years old. I don't understand how this time will be any different. The migraine pain a few times a month is not as difficult as the daily struggle to avoid foods that I want for comfort. Pessimistic, I decide to be tested for food allergies. The first test is a collection of a few days of poop samples. A more precise test is a blood sample, which costs a few hundred dollars. I start with the poop.

Ultimately I don't want to fear food. I don't want to fear my immune system. I don't want to fear anything – not wheat or dairy, not pharmaceuticals, petrochemicals, electromagnetic waves, "bad energy." I am on a spiritual quest to manage fear, but I find the alternative health, new age, woo-woo world just as neurotic and frightened as the rest of society. I want to be the Buddha in hell. I don't want to have to manage my external world to have internal peace. If my moment-to-moment okayness is dependent on any external circumstance, I will forever be expending energy outside myself; adjusting a world I ultimately have little control over. My energy is better spent on internal peace, on smoothing and releasing my state of mind, my perspectives and attitudes, where I have some control. I have an inkling that I may be whole and okay exactly as I am, I believe it about eighty percent of the time.

During this time I flash between old habits of mind and new. I feel fat, plan new diets, and dream about being thin for a trip to Hawaii at Christmas. While I move through these old habits of mind one part is different: my awareness of what I am doing. I *notice* I am carrying out old habits. I still do it, but am slightly removed from it. I have a new confidence, an ever-present grounding. People around me seem sped up and anxious, living in the head. I experience them like a calm observer, like an alien visiting here, taking an unhurried look around, unaffected by all the frenetic activity. No matter what I am feeling, thinking, or what is going on, the quiet is always there, available to me. I know it is there, a deeper me, a more fundamental, larger Keelin, even as I hover above it in my own pain or anxiety. I know I will be in the quiet again sometime. This will pass.

I learn to comfort myself: *I can be afraid and be here. I can be sick and be here. I can be overweight and be here. I can be out of balance and be here. It does not matter. What evolves will evolve.* All I have to do is say yes, move into expansion and resist contraction, pay attention, relax and surrender.

I have three cats from the same litter, two females and their brother. They are eight years old. We leave for a weekend trip to Tahoe and a few days after our return, Sophie, our favorite, suddenly falls ill. Her liver has failed. Rather than put her in the hospital with a feeding tube, we decide to put her down. I experience this loss in an entirely new way than any previous loss in my life. I feel joyful, and awed that I could feel this way at this time. I love Sophie and I told her about it every day. I have no feelings of being cheated by her death. She trusted me to care for her, to not put her through medical procedures that would not improve her comfort or joy in living. I sense her work here is complete. She is ready for her next assignment. And what a beautiful job she did in her little cat form. She was a gift to us and deserves blessings and peace.

My parents divorced when I was about two years old. From about age five to age twelve, every summer, I travelled by myself on airplanes from central Illinois to Los Angeles and back again. For seven years of my childhood, almost every year, when I went to California, my father would have moved to a new place, and when I returned to Illinois, my mother would have moved. Whenever I travel as an adult, I experience a disabling anxiety that something will be lost if I leave home. This Tahoe trip was anxiety free. The week I am back, I experience an actual loss, my beloved cat dies, and my overriding feeling is of gratitude for the time I had with her – no dread, no fear of more loss, no guilt or self-punishment thoughts for going on the trip. Amazing.

I finish Blue Fire, at least the formal, twenty-one sessions of loosely structured Original Design Inquiry, at the end of March. In gratitude, I make a gate for Anna. About a foot high, two cedar twigs, embedded in a hunk of wood, cross to create a doorway. I hang a small, vertical, flat piece of coastal hemlock bark on copper wire hinges, with a tiny latch. After my last session, I write Anna an email: 4/2/08

> Went to Tahoe last week... it is so beautiful there! I brought back this pile of rocks and driftwood – none of which has any purpose whatsoever. It was all just talking to me so I kept putting it in my pockets. We went hiking in the desert... I picked up this small green rock. Carried it around. And it was so noisy, like I'd picked up an electron cloud in my hand. And I wondered if I should look for another rock there and the green one told me yeah, a red one. But there weren't any red rocks anywhere so I just kept walking and sure enough, there was a red one. It was less talkative, but amazingly beautiful, like a piece of the desert – layers of light sand and red sand with darker lines and cracks.
>
> I continue to be amazed at how easily I float along in life now. I am so easygoing I find I cannot even be bothered to express how infinitely grateful I am to YOU AND THE GUIDES AND BLUE FIRE. You, they, me – did something to me that it appears I might get to keep. I am still testing the waters... how long do I get to be this person? This being that knows deeply ALL IS RIGHT. Everything is just as it should be right now. So I relax, pay some gentle attention, do what feels right, and don't do anything more. I am still on this expansive wave I have been on for a while. I can be this person who experiences human things, like illness, pain, fear, jealousy, insecurity, disappointment, envy, greed, grief (grief? I cannot remember that one right now but I am sure I have felt it at some point :)!), and I just tell myself, "I can be afraid, petty, sad, etc. and still be here." Powerful words.
>
> I feel mainly that Blue Fire set me free. All I want to do is evolve. I'm addicted and I have no control over any of it and that doesn't matter. I just know it is there, always, no matter if I feel it or not, and that if I just relax, I can participate more fully. Everything else is just here too, along for the ride, interesting, irritating, beautiful... but peripheral to the intense pleasure of expansion. I feel surrounded by others' need to

confine, define, struggle and feel inadequate. I just watch, but I don't feel inadequate, or fundamentally ill, anymore. **It is like healing is not really about changing anything manifest in this world – healing is about letting go of the idea that we need healing.** The healing that may occur comes from surrender, from the willingness to not define what life should be.

And I am almost so secure that I don't care if anyone else understands or believes me (almost :)). My husband would call that the definition of insanity, but as Rita once told me, as long as I can guess what day it is and who is the president and remember to put my clothes on before getting on the bus, I am sane enough for this world.

Much, much love and rejoicing my dear Anna…

Blue Fire teaches me I am home. I have a lightness in my head, an emptiness, peace of mind. I become a fierce defender of my wholeness. The wound is closed and healed and I refuse to open it again by volunteering to gouge out pieces with doubt and fear. I believe in my wholeness blindly, without question. The world's or my own imperfections are part of the whole. Most of the time, things no longer appear to me as deficient or needy. I no longer feel inadequate, like something is missing. Most of the time I accept the now as enough, as it is, and am able to do or not do what feels right in the moment, what I can do within all my perfect imperfection. One day in April, I wake from a dream with the chorus from "She's Come Undone" in my head. I go downstairs to my computer and write a poem:

I'm coming undone
unraveled, unspun

my body spilling open
intestines unwound

stretching glottis to appendix, marveling
at all the room
organs uncoil, dance a jig
stomach and liver clap in time
spleen and pancreas do-si-do

a taste of freedom now there's no going back
nauseated, I can't keep my ducklings in a row
I count, I count... is one missing? nothing lines up

mouse says he wants to help
whiskers a-quiver, feeling his way, feather by feather
earnest, honest
he doesn't know he can't see over the yellow-feather heads

unbound, my dream is all Furies
I rage at my mother to turn the car around
my husband fell out
he's hurt, I've lost him
but I love you, I love you!
there's no more keeping it in

unwounded, I gently unfurl
petals tender in the brightness lightness

all done, undone
all that's left to do is to
relax, unwind

the work of holding me up doesn't need doing
I melt, puddle across the paving stones
seep into the moss and sand

ecstatically scrubbed clean in the sieve of earth and stone
I don't end anymore
I begin everywhere and we

we gather in rivulets, runnels,
streaming to fuel the universe.

Suggested Reading

For a translation of Siddhartha Gautama Buddha's *The Dhammapada* see webpage: www.davar.net/ZEN/DHAMAPAD.HTM. Quoted passage is in "9. Mischief".

Bradley, Allison. 2006. "The Blue Fire Project." See webpage: www.bluefireproject.org.

Campbell, Joseph, with Bill Moyers. 1988. *The Power of Myth*. New York: Doubleday.

Cameron, Anne. 1981. *Daughters of Copper Woman*. Madeira Park, BC, Canada: Harbour Publishing.

Douglass, Sara. 1999. *Crusader*. New York: Tom Doherty Associates.

——. 1996. *Starman*. New York: Tom Doherty Associates.

——. 1995. *The Wayfarer Redemption*. New York: Tom Doherty Associates.

Fusselman, Amy. 2007. "Feet to Brain." See webpage: www.nytimes.com/2007/04/15/magazine/15lives.t.html.

Golomb, Elan. 1992. *Trapped in the Mirror*. New York: William Morrow.

Haines, Staci. 1999. *The Survivor's Guide to Sex: How to Have An Empowered Sex Life After Childhood Sexual Abuse*. San Francisco: Cleis Press.

Harner, Michael. 1980. *The Way of the Shaman*. San Francisco: Harper Collins.

Hirsch, Edward. 2006. *Poet's Choice*. Orlando: Harcourt.

Levin, Daniel. 2001. *Zen Cards*. Carlsbad: Hay House.

Longfellow, Henry Wadsworth. "The Wreck of the Hesperus". See webpage: www.blupete.com/Literature/Poetry/Wreck.htm.

Mahasattva Swami Krishna Prem, et. al. 1983. *Rajneesh Neo-Tarot*. Rajneeshpuram, OR: Rajneesh Foundation International.

McKinley, Robin. 2003. *Sunshine*. New York: The Berkley Publishing Group.

Milne, Hugh. 1995. *The Heart of Listening, Volume I*. Berkeley: North Atlantic Books.

Myss, Caroline. 1996. *Anatomy of the Spirit: The Seven Stages of Power and Healing*. New York: Three Rivers Press.

———. 2003. *Sacred Contracts: Awakening Your Divine Potential*. New York: Three Rivers Press.

Oliver, Mary. 2003. *Owls and Other Fantasies*. Boston: Beacon Press.

Pullman, Philip. 2000. *The Amber Spyglass*. New York: Laurel-Leaf.

———. 1997. *The Subtle Knife*. New York: Laurel-Leaf.

Sams, Jamie and David Carson. 1988. *Medicine Cards*. New York: St. Martin's Press.

Trungpa, Chogyam. 1984. *Shambhala: The Sacred Path of the Warrior*. Boston: Shambhala Publications.

Williamson, Marianne. 1992. *A Return to Love, Reflections of the Principles of A COURSE IN MIRACLES*. New York: HarperCollins.

Wilson, C.L. 2007. *Lady of Light and Shadows*. New York, Dorchester Publishing.